On the cover: **THE IRVINGTON DEPOT, 1880.** The Irvington depot was located on Depot Avenue east of Audubon Road and south of the George W. Julian home. The station was built in 1873 as the first commercial structure in Irvington. The railroad provided the primary form of travel to and from the suburban community in the town's early days, and the station remained in service until 1922. It was demolished in 1925. (Courtesy of Indiana Historical Society.)

IMAGES
of America

HISTORIC IRVINGTON

Julie Young

ARCADIA
PUBLISHING

Published by Arcadia Publishing
Charleston, South Carolina

Library of Congress Catalog Card Number: 2008920513

For all general information contact Arcadia Publishing at:
Telephone 843-853-2070
Fax 843-853-0044
E-mail sales@arcadiapublishing.com
For customer service and orders:
Toll-Free 1-888-313-2665

Visit us on the Internet at www.arcadiapublishing.com

This book is dedicated to Chris, Vincent, and members of my own Johnson family who lived or worked in Irvington and inspired my love of the community and its people.

CONTENTS

Acknowledgments   6

Introduction   7

1.   A Peek into the Past   9

2.   The Butler Connection   25

3.   A Cornucopia of Design   45

4.   Irvington Congregations   61

5.   Inside the Classroom   81

6.   The People   99

7.   The Landmarks   113

Bibliography   127

ACKNOWLEDGMENTS

This book has been a unique opportunity for me, and I am eternally grateful to every member of the Irvington community who responded to countless telephone calls and e-mails, spread the word, and shared their private photograph collections for this volume. Without you, this project could never have been completed. A special thank-you goes out to Don Flick and the Irvington Historical Society, Marge Conly, Bea Cottom, Carolyn Wyatt, Howard Caldwell Jr., the Indiana Historical Society, Sally Childs-Helton at Butler University, and the gals at the Sleepy Hollow. Your support has made all the difference.

Thank you to every writer who has taken the time to talk to me, give me advice, be a role model, and encourage me to follow my dreams, including Elizabeth Berg, Emily Giffin, Judy Blume, and of course, Gene Simmons. You are right; every day above ground really is a good day.

Thank you to Anna Wilson and everyone at Arcadia Publishing; it has been a pleasure working with you, and I appreciate your time and patience especially during the tension-filled early weeks of this project. Somehow it always works out; I am just never sure how.

Aunt Sandy Denton, thank you for sharing so many of your Irvington stories with me and opening my eyes to the community. Over the years, Irvington became a second home to me, whether it was walking to the corner store on Audubon Road for a Slush Puppie, enjoying cookouts in your backyard, watching the Howe High School band, or initiating my love of Butler University. Your family really helped me embrace the Irvington spirit.

Finally, and most importantly, to the guys, who never seem surprised by my next big idea and who persistently remind me that "normal is vastly overrated." You are my constant inspiration.

INTRODUCTION

The town of Irvington was conceived during the Victorian Gilded Age, when men in stiff collars tipped their hats to corseted ladies on their way to "pay a call" at one of the charming Second Empire or Queen Anne–style homes. It was a time when the soft clop of horse hooves and the low wail of a train whistle dominated transportation trends long before the rumble of automobile engines. It was the precursor to the Edwardian era but the beginning of a sense of security for the upper middle classes who had complete faith in the future and believed that things were only getting better with time.

When Quaker abolitionists Jacob Julian and Sylvester Johnson sought to create a community that would serve as a suburb to a large metropolis while having its own separate identity in 1870, they could not have known the impact that the historic town of Irvington would have on the east side of Indianapolis over a century later.

From the winding curvilinear streets to the rich diversity of architecture representing every major period of style from 1870 to 1950, Irvington is a unique area that serves as a time capsule for those who live there today. Irvington in the late 19th century was a community ahead of its time. Covenants designed to restrict the sale of alcohol, the erection of slaughterhouses, the manufacturing of soap and other noxious pollutants, along with ordinances that required the planting of trees, established Irvington at the forefront of planned, environmentally friendly communities. Other plans called for the inclusion of a women's college and the establishment of a public park. These were progressive goals at the time, but it was that promise of progress that made Irvington attractive to the well read, scholarly group of citizens that initially resided in the area.

Although it was annexed into Indianapolis in 1902, Irvington still kept its identity as its own community with a quiet neighborhood atmosphere. Today Irvington is the largest locally protected historic district in Indianapolis and includes about 1,600 buildings and 1,900 parcels of land within the historic area. It is currently home to approximately 10,000 residents.

When North Western Christian University, a coeducational institution, needed a new home in 1873, Irvington was only too happy to provide the expanding university with plenty of land to create the college town the community longed for. A new building was constructed to house the school, and North Western Christian University moved to Irvington in 1875, changing its name to Butler University. Although most of the school buildings were demolished and the land was used to create more housing in the area, the Bona Thompson Memorial Library, built in 1903 (now the Bona Thompson Memorial Center), remains. Homes where students boarded, or places that served as fraternity, sorority, and faculty residences, such as the Benton House, still dot the Irvington landscape as a ghost of the town's academic past even though the days as a vibrant college community are long gone.

As Irvington was able to incorporate more economic development into the landscape, the area drew many notables, including Kin Hubbard, who was famous for his "Abe Martin" cartoon character; Layton Allen, a well-respected architect who designed several homes in the area; and civic, educational, and longtime newspaperman Hilton U. Brown. Among the famous were the infamous as well, including early mass murderer Dr. H. H. Holmes, who was responsible for the death of 10-year-old Howard Pitezel in a rented Victorian cottage on Julian Avenue. Legendary gangster John Dillinger once used Irvington as a hideout, and a prominent drugstore in the area served as the backdrop for one of his early robberies. The most infamous Irvington resident, David Curtis (D. C.) Stephenson, served as the grand dragon of the Ku Klux Klan and was said to have been running Indiana politics from the comfort of his Irvington mansion.

Irvington is also known for a number of independently owned and operated businesses in the area primarily located along the Washington Street corridor. There are a number of small stores that have taken over what was once a thriving Main Street and revitalized the storefronts to bring bookstores, gift shops, restaurants, and antique dealers to the area.

Major employers in the surrounding community include Community Hospital East, Navistar, and Indy Parks, which is responsible for the upkeep of Ellenberger Park. Established in 1911, the park formalized the use of the land that had long been a recreation site for the community. Other notable landmarks in the community include the former College of Missions, several churches, a thriving public library, and the Marion County Children's Guardians Home.

Despite the grandeur of its early days, the latter part of the 20th century was hard on Irvington. The advent of interstate systems and shopping centers drove businesses and residents away from the community, leaving the Main Street boarded and historic homes out of touch with a changing world. The Irving Theatre is one such casualty. Built in 1913, the movie house fell on hard times in the early 1970s but was renewed as a family theater in the late 1980s. It closed in the mid-1990s due to the pressure of multiplex theaters that offered customers more choices for their admission price. Today the Irving serves as a live music venue, and it has once again become a cultural epicenter of the community.

Education in Irvington is as diverse as its people. Thomas Carr Howe High School enjoyed a proud tradition in academics before closing its doors in 1995 due to declining enrollment. However, the school reopened in 2000 as an Indianapolis Public Schools academy. School 85 was also involved in area redistricting and has since been converted into an office building. The establishment of the Irvington Community Charter School along with the presence of school 57 and Our Lady of Lourdes Catholic School provide Irvington residents with a wide variety of learning institutions.

Thanks to the diligence of longtime members of the Irvington community and the city of Indianapolis, Irvington in the 21st century is once again the "place to be." Residents are encouraged to shop local, support the neighborhood organizations, and celebrate that small-town feel. Today Irvington residents are proud of their heritage, and they show it throughout the year with various events that Irvington celebrates. The best-known and oldest celebration is the Halloween festival. Once a year, East Washington Street is closed through downtown Irvington to hold the festival. This event attracts many vendors and also gives local politicians the opportunity to campaign and meet with their constituents. Also Irvington businesses, churches, and organizations construct booths so that neighbors can learn more about them. The festival traditionally concludes with a costumed parade. Other events during the year include the Celebrate Irvington weekend in June, a farmer's market held throughout the summer, the Benton House Tour of Homes, and the old-fashioned ice-cream social at the Bona Thompson Center. During the Christmas season, a spectacular luminaria display lights up streets throughout the community.

Recognized as a national historic district, Irvington is the kind of town that preserves its past while pressing on into the future.

One

A PEEK INTO THE PAST

When Quaker abolitionists Jacob Julian and Sylvester Johnson grew disenchanted with politics in their home community of Centerville, the pair dreamed of the day that they could create an autonomous community that would serve as a suburb to a nearby larger city. Five miles east of downtown Indianapolis, they found the perfect place, and the two purchased a 320-acre tenant farm for $100 an acre.

The acreage was perfectly situated along the National Road and bracketed by two railroads providing plenty of transportation opportunities to those who inhabited the new and unnamed town.

Julian and Johnson's original 1870 plat shows that their community consisted of 109 two-acre lots capped off with a curvilinear street pattern and provisions in place for a future female college and public park.

Julian bestowed the name Irvington on the town in honor of his favorite writer, Washington Irving, but as it turned out, Irving was not the only writer honored in the new community. Several streets within the town bore the names of famous wordsmiths, including John Greenleaf Whittier, Nathaniel Hawthorne, and Ralph Waldo Emerson.

Johnson's contribution to the town was the provision in all the deeds that prohibited the sale of alcohol within the town limits, which is still examined regularly when new businesses arrive to the area. However, a financial panic in 1873 caused a setback to the new community, resulting in the subdivision of some lots and driving Julian into near bankruptcy.

Although one of the founders left Irvington in its infancy, the town began a steady growth as physicians and grocery stores began establishing themselves around the railroad depot. Religious communities flourished, too, and a school system was also implemented in those early years.

However, due to increased municipal needs and a lack of options for funding them, some residents petitioned Indianapolis for annexation. It was granted in 1902, giving Irvington the opportunity for better roads, protection from fire, and a city water supply.

Whether alone or as part of Indianapolis, Irvington was on its way to becoming a hub of activity on the east side, solidifying its reputation for the better part of the 20th century.

IRVINGTON, 1881. The earliest-known photograph of the town was taken in 1881 from the tower of Irvington's first public school. In the upper left corner is the home of Dr. Levi Ritter, located at present-day Ritter Avenue and Washington Street. He owned the parcel of land adjacent to Irvington, which became the town's first addition. The home to the right of the Ritter house is the only house still extant. (Courtesy of Larry Muncie.)

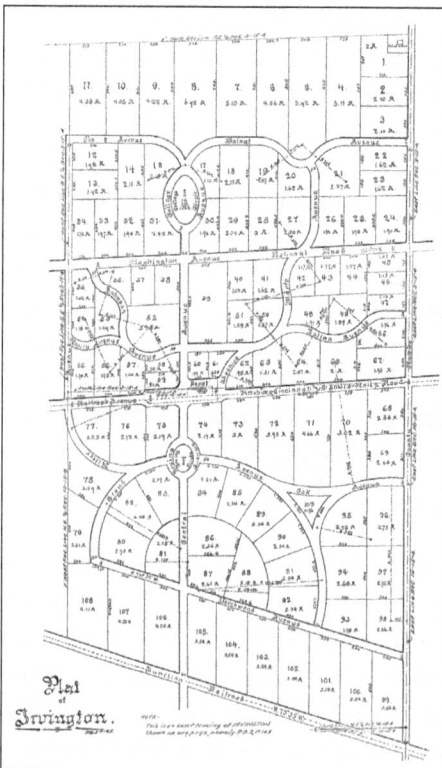

ORIGINAL PLAT OF IRVINGTON, 1870. Irvington architect Don Dick drew this rendering of the original plat of Irvington to commemorate the town's centennial. It includes the original designs for lots and the winding street pattern, which some claimed was created by following a meandering cow. After the financial panic in 1873, many of the lots were subdivided to help Irvington remain an attractive option for prospective property owners. (Courtesy of Irvington Historical Society Archives.)

JACOB JULIAN WITH HIS FAMILY. Irvington cofounder Jacob Julian (third row, right) poses for a photograph with his family. He was known for his work as Wayne County prosecutor as well as serving as a bank president and as a member of the state legislature before joining with Sylvester Johnson to develop the plan that became Irvington. The two built grand homes across the street from one another, but Julian lived in Irvington for only a short time due to financial problems and later moved to Indianapolis. In exchange for Johnson's desire not to have alcohol sold within the town's limits, Julian was given the honor of naming the town after his favorite writer, Washington Irving, a name that was suggested by his daughter. The present street just south of the National Road in Irvington bears Julian's name. (Courtesy of Larry Muncie.)

THE NATIONAL ROAD TOLLHOUSE, 1850–1890. There were two tollhouses located near Irvington that were operated by the Central Plank Road Company in order to fund improvements along the National Road. This house was located just west of Irvington, while the other was situated east of Sheridan Avenue. As improvements occurred, including the installation of trolley rails, the tollhouses were no longer needed and were removed from service. (Courtesy of Larry Muncie.)

THE ELLENBERGER FAMILY, C. 1882. John Ellenberger (seated, center) moved his family to the Irvington area from Cincinnati in 1853. He farmed the land as a tenant and eventually bought acreage that he farmed north of the future town. A portion of his land, known as Ellenberger Woods, ultimately became Ellenberger Park. The home still stands at 5602 East Tenth Street. (Courtesy of Larry Muncie.)

THE NATIONAL ROAD, C. 1910. This early scene along the north side of U.S. Route 40 is looking west from Ritter Avenue. Although the area around the railroad depot provided the initial commercial opportunities, the advent of the trolley and automobiles made sites along the National Road more desirable for development. From left to right are Karnes Grocery, the Irvington Fire Station, Irvington Ford Sales, and the Irvington Meat Market. (Courtesy of Larry Muncie.)

EAST WASHINGTON STREET POSTCARD. A later view along the north side of the street west of Ritter Avenue shows the National Road, or Washington Street, paved and with more businesses having located along U.S. Route 40. Also in view is a portion of the buildings on the northeast corner of the intersection. Only the building on the right with the awning stands today. (Courtesy of Don and Lisa Flick.)

13

IRVINGTON TRAIN DEPOT, 1883. Seen here in 1883, the Irvington train depot served not only as a train station but also as a post office, meeting room, and polling station over the years. The railroad line that ran through the original commercial center of Irvington was known as the Panhandle Line before it became the Pennsylvania Railroad around the start of the 20th century. (Courtesy of Larry Muncie.)

SIGNAL CONTROL TOWER. Named "the shanty" by local residents, this control tower for the Pennsylvania Railroad was operated by a watchman 24 hours a day. (Courtesy of Robert Montgomery.)

IRVING CIRCLE PARK, C. 1906. This photograph shows the original fountain located in the center of Irving Circle Park at present-day Audubon Road and University Avenue. Plans originally included the fountain, which was erected in the late 1800s, and the bust of Washington Irving. (Courtesy of Larry Muncie.)

ORIGINAL BUST OF WASHINGTON IRVING. More than 50 years after Irvington was named in his honor, a bust of Washington Irving by sculptor William Kriner was installed in Irving Circle Park on September 9, 1936. Kriner worked on the bust for three months. The statue now stands on the grounds of school 57 at the corner of Washington Street and Ritter Avenue. (Photograph by R. Cole; courtesy of Larry Muncie.)

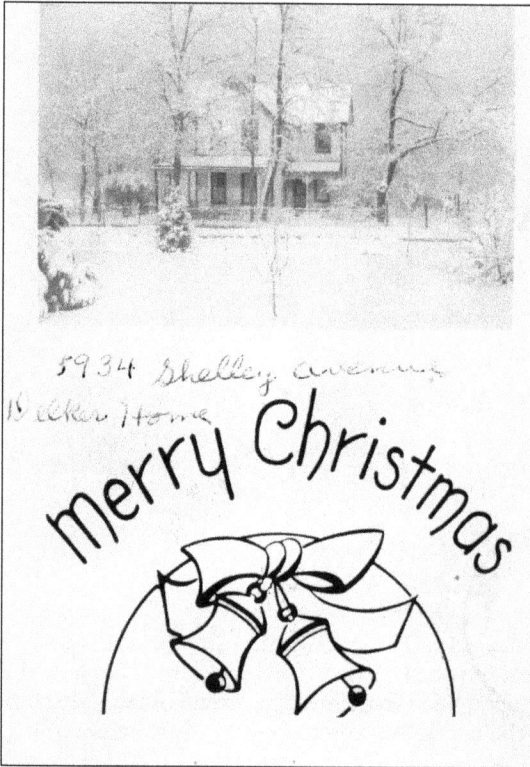

REAL-PHOTO POSTCARD OF IRVINGTON HOME. This postcard depicts the Delker home located at 5934 Shelley Avenue in Irvington. Penny postcards that featured homes or people offered personal touches to the holidays, and many Irvington residents capitalized on the idea of having their private photograph collections made into postcards for correspondence. (Courtesy of Mark and Cathy Kippert.)

DOWNEY AVENUE WITH BRICK STREETS. This photograph shows a typical residential area in Irvington complete with many shade trees. One of the early plans for the community was to incorporate several large trees. Many of these trees are still part of the landscape today. (Courtesy of Larry Muncie.)

16

THE MOUNT ZION SCHOOL, 1892. Early records show that there were some subscription schools in the area that became Irvington as early as 1846. The Mount Zion Township School offered one of the earliest educational opportunities for children living in Irvington until the town's public school was built. It was organized in the 1850s as a Sunday school in a one-room cabin, and this photograph shows the student body and structure after the school was relocated to Sixteenth Street and Arlington Avenue. From the moment of the town's inception, there was almost a constant need for educational facilities. Although the Mount Zion School, too, was originally a subscription school, it became a public institution once Indiana law required free education. When the Irvington public school was built, Mount Zion lost a lot of its students. (Courtesy of Larry Muncie.)

THE FIRST IRVINGTON PUBLIC SCHOOL, 1898. The first Irvington public school opened in October 1874. The structure was designed as a one-room brick structure but eventually expanded to a three-story building on the southeast corner of Audubon Road and University Avenue opposite Irving Circle. It had an enrollment of 330 children with eight teachers. On December 16, 1898, an overheated furnace caused a fire that destroyed the school. The above photograph was taken at approximately 2:00 a.m. from the tower of the Eudorus Johnson home across the street from the school, while the photograph below shows the ruins the morning after the tragedy. The second Irvington school was built south of the site of the fire and opened on September 25, 1899. That school, too, burned down in 1903. (Courtesy of Larry Muncie.)

CHILDREN PLAYING ON BOARDWALKS, C. 1890. In the late 1890s, boardwalks lined the streets of Irvington before annexation paved the way for brick streets. New homeowners wanted sidewalks and city water, prompting some Irvington residents to seek annexation by Indianapolis in 1902. Annexation gave Irvington an improved school system, sewage lines, and lower taxes and insurance rates, as well as improved property values. (Courtesy of Larry Muncie.)

CHILDREN ON PAVING BRICKS, 1907. A group of unidentified children on Ritter Avenue play on the paving bricks stacked along the road in 1907. In the years that followed annexation, promised improvements to the Irvington community were slow in coming, and as a result, streets were riddled with weeds and the sidewalks were neglected. (Courtesy of Larry Muncie.)

PLEASANT RUN, 1898. Pleasant Run was a popular place for family picnics and fishing excursions. Five-year-old Sidney Hecker fishes in the local creek. Note the dress, as it was common for boys to wear dresses in the Victorian era until they were old enough to wear knickers. (Courtesy of Larry Muncie.)

THE PLEASANT RUN SWIMMING HOLE. Although the date of this photograph is unknown, it shows a group of Irvington children cooling off on a hot summer's day. Today the creek is still a popular attraction for visitors to Ellenberger Park, although modern aquatic facilities and health concerns make wading in Pleasant Run less desirable. (Courtesy of Larry Muncie.)

RITTER AVENUE IN WINTER, 1905. This 1905 photograph of an unidentified woman and child playing in the snow was taken on Ritter Avenue just north of Washington Street. The homes visible in the background are 31 and 39 North Ritter Avenue. The photograph was taken after the annexation into Indianapolis but before Ritter Avenue was paved. (Courtesy of Larry Muncie.)

RITTER AVENUE IN SPRING, 1907. This 1907 photograph shows a woman and child (probably the same two as in the above photograph) taking their baby carriage for a walk in Irvington. Note the telephone lines. In 1900, the Central Union Telephone Company offered home service to Irvington residents from a line that ran to 520 North Ritter Avenue where the exchange board was located in the home of Hamilton Cooper. (Courtesy of Larry Muncie.)

MIMI AND THE PONY. Two-year-old Mimi Roseman, aunt of Lori Malander, sits astride what was known as the "Irvington pony." According to family stories, the "pony man" came into Irvington and set up with his pony at Irving Circle Park in addition to other locations around the east side. It was popular for children to get their picture taken astride the pony on their birthdays or at other times of the year if it was prearranged. (Courtesy of Lori Malander.)

WALKING TOUR, 1970S. Walking tours have always been a way that Irvington residents celebrate their past. From the Benton House Tour of Homes in the early fall that celebrates the architecture and design of Irvington to open houses and self-guided tours of the landmarks around the neighborhood, various groups create unique and different ways to approach Irvington's historic past and make it relevant for a younger generation. This photograph shows members of the Downey Avenue Christian Church stopping at the former home of Effie Cunningham on one of the walking tours. The woman in the rocker on the porch is Leta Bradney portraying Cunningham, the editor of the *Missionary Tidings*, later known as *World Call*. Bradney is shown holding a copy of a 1919 edition of the magazine. (Courtesy of Downey Avenue Christian Church.)

THE CARRIAGE RIDE. The photograph above shows a group of unidentified Irvington women driving north on Ritter Avenue after paving was completed in 1907. The number of white dresses could indicate that the photograph was taken in late spring or early summer. Below, a second unidentified group of Irvington matrons and children head out for a drive on Ritter Avenue in their open carriage, posing for a picture along the way. Although there were still many women who declined to drive their own carriages in the early 20th century, these ladies clearly embraced their independence as progressive members of Irvington society. (Courtesy of Larry Muncie.)

Two

THE BUTLER
CONNECTION

Although Jacob Julian and Sylvester Johnson hoped to add a female college or seminary to their new community in the future, an opportunity presented itself in 1873 when North Western Christian University needed to expand from its downtown Indianapolis location. Irvington jumped at the chance to bring the campus to the east side, and the town immediately offered 25 acres of land and $150,000 to make it happen.

The institution was named Butler University in honor of Ovid Butler, an Indianapolis attorney and the school's founder. In 1874, ground was broken on the first of several academic structures to dot the Irvington landscape.

Butler University helped Irvington achieve its desire to be a cultural leader in the city by offering plays and lectures that locals often attended. The presence of the university gave Irvington an amenity that other communities simply could not compete with. Not only did educated professionals invest in the college town by building grand homes, but Butler University also became a major benefactor to the town, helping various entities obtain money for needed improvements.

As early as 1902, Butler University's administration saw that the Irvington campus offered limited possibilities. Two adjacent railroad lines were not conducive to a studious atmosphere, and by the end of World War I, with a burgeoning enrollment, the school had an immediate need to expand again.

The school's faculty became the crème de la crème of Irvington, and many of their homes along Downey Avenue and elsewhere in the community still stand along with several homes that served as fraternity and sorority houses. The academic feel of Irvington was augmented when the College of Missions opened in 1910, providing training for missionaries for work domestically and overseas.

The university considered moving to Columbus, Indiana, but decided to set its sights on the north side of Indianapolis. The last Butler graduation in Irvington took place in 1928. The vacated buildings sat empty, and by 1939, most of the original Butler buildings were demolished with the exception of the Bona Thompson Memorial Library, which today serves as the headquarters for the Irvington Historical Society and stands as a tribute to Irvington's life as a college town.

NORTH WESTERN CHRISTIAN UNIVERSITY POSTCARD. Located at Thirteenth Street and College Avenue in downtown Indianapolis, North Western Christian University was the precursor to Butler University. In 1873, administrators saw a need to expand the campus, and Irvington officials saw the school as an opportunity to bring higher education to the east side. (Courtesy of Don and Lisa Flick.)

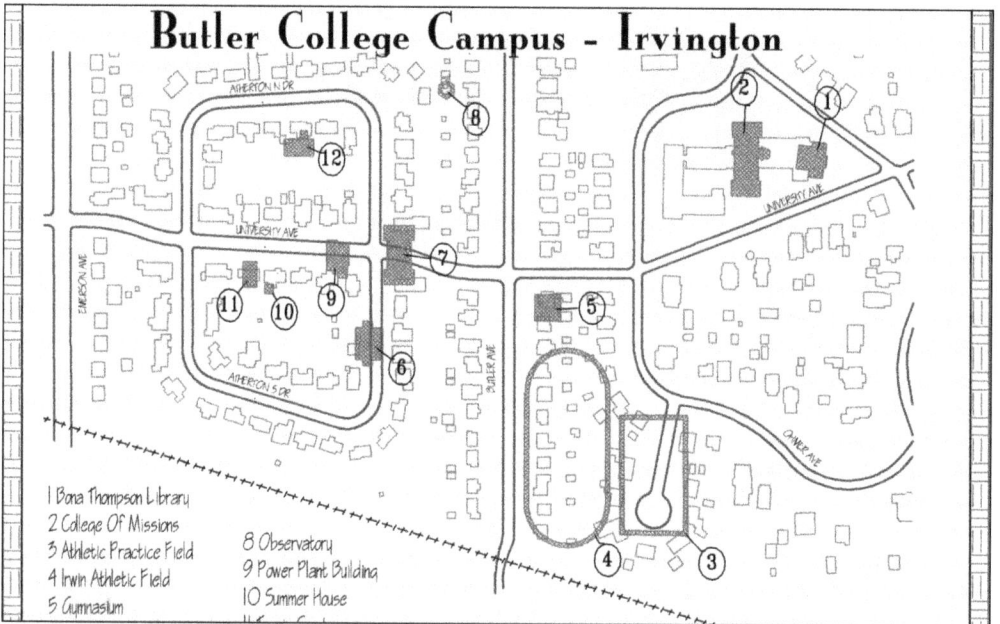

MAP OF BUTLER COLLEGE. This map of Butler's Irvington campus is superimposed on today's neighborhood. In addition to the academic buildings, there were many faculty homes and Greek houses throughout Irvington. When the college moved to the east side, many families built or bought homes in the area so their children could attend the college. (Courtesy of Irvington Historical Society Archives.)

BUTLER UNIVERSITY MAIN BUILDING. In 1875, classes commenced at the main building on Butler's Irvington campus. Although the building was never named, in addition to classrooms and administrative offices, the structure contained a chapel, a library, and meeting spaces within its brick walls. The building cost more than $15,000 to erect and was accessed by students via railroads, mule-drawn trolleys, or by walking. Butler University was not only the cultural epicenter of the town but its professors often served on the town board. Affiliated with the Christian Church (Disciples of Christ), many professors also acted as ministers in the local Christian Church. In fact, before the first Christian Church building was erected in Irvington, Butler's main building was the site of religious services for many years. (Above, courtesy of Larry Muncie; below, courtesy of the Irvington Historical Society Archives.)

SUMMER HOUSE AND WEST VIEW OF CAMPUS. The western view of the Butler University campus offered lush green spaces and plenty of shade trees in harmony with the rest of the Irvington landscape. The stone boulder Summer House west of the main building offered students a place where they could conduct small gatherings, watch a tennis match, or find shelter during a rainstorm. By today's standard, Butler's Irvington campus was very small and offered few amenities, but at the time, Butler in many ways set the bar for the kind of facilities many colleges and universities aspired to. (Above, courtesy of Irvington Historical Society; below, photograph by Frank Jones, courtesy of Downey Avenue Christian Church.)

WEST CAMPUS
BUTLER COLLEGE

BURGESS HALL. Located south of the main building, the science building was named for Otis Burgess, who served as Butler's president from 1873 to 1881. He believed that if women wanted to prove their equality to men in the academic field, they should be allowed to do so. During his tenure, the difference in curriculum between genders was abolished. (Courtesy of Larry Muncie.)

BONA THOMPSON MEMORIAL LIBRARY. The Bona Thompson Memorial Library is the only Butler College building that was not demolished after the school relocated. Completed in 1903 as the last permanent structure on the campus, the library was named for the late Bona Thompson, an 1897 Butler graduate. Her parents donated $40,000 as well as the land at Downey and University Avenues for the building. (Courtesy of Larry Muncie.)

BUTLER GRADUATING CLASS, 1878. This photograph of one of the earliest graduating classes on the Irvington Butler campus included (first row) Ernest R. Copeland and Katharine Merrill Graydon; (second row) Bizzanna O' Connor (Sister Ariana), Oliver Romeo Johnson, Albert Bayard Kirkpatrick, and Charles Edgar Thornton. (Courtesy of Irvington Historical Society Archives.)

BUTLER FACULTY, C. 1910. This photograph shows a distinguished panel of educators who were on staff during Butler's years in Irvington. From left to right are (first row) Christopher Bush Coleman, Myrtle Lewellyn Taylor, unidentified, Thomas Carr Howe, Jabez Hall, Katharine Merrill Graydon, and Elijah Newton Johnson; (second row) Edward Martin Greene, Edmund Howard Hollands, Cornelia Adelle Allen, James William Putnam, and Henry Mills Gelston; (third row) John McKay, John Samuel Kenyon, unidentified, and George Henry Danton. (Courtesy of Larry Muncie.)

IRWIN FIELD, BUTLER COLLEGE CAMPUS. The athletic field was located on the east side of Butler Avenue south of University Avenue. The land was purchased in 1905 by William Irwin, who also provided funds for the layout of the football field, a quarter-mile track, and the erection of spectator stands. Irwin Field offered a combination of athletic events, including football, baseball, and track. Although sports at the Irvington campus were limited, Butler possessed one of the best athletic fields in the state, and as many as 10,000 fans came to watch the various events. (Courtesy of Indiana Historical Society Bass Collection.)

BUTLER COLLEGE FOOTBALL TEAM. The exact date that Butler introduced a football program is disputed, but when "the Butler eleven" was organized, it had the benefit of Yale University graduate Evans Woollen on the coaching staff, who understood the fundamentals of the game and gave the team an edge over rivals. (Courtesy of Don and Lisa Flick.)

FEMALE DORMITORY BUTLER UNIVERSITY. Many of Butler's students found nearby homes in which to board or joined Greek houses in order to secure a residence. However, the university did add a dormitory on the north side of the campus. The residence was designed as a coeducational dormitory, but in 1893, the building was reserved exclusively for women. (Photograph by Frank Jones, courtesy of Downey Avenue Christian Church.)

THE BUTLER ASSOCIATION, 1923. The Butler Association, a fraternal organization within the Butler community, was located at 5342 East Washington Street. Its motto was "Soulful Soloing." The house has been razed, and the Moore and Kirk Funeral Home is now on the site. (Photograph by Frank Jones, courtesy of Butler University.)

DELTA TAU DELTA, 1923. Many of the Butler College fraternity and sorority homes changed locations from year to year. Now demolished, this house at 15 South Ritter Avenue served as the home of Delta Tau Delta in 1923. In the background, the Irvington Masonic Lodge building is visible. (Photograph by Frank Jones, courtesy of Butler University.)

DELTA TAU DELTA REUNION, CLAYPOOL HOTEL, INDIANAPOLIS. One of Butler's oldest fraternities was Delta Tau Delta, which boarded its members in at least two Irvington houses (since razed) over the years at 15 South Ritter Avenue and 5342 East Washington Street. Because family members often pledged the same fraternity or sorority, the Hall and Glass families had at least 21 members who were Delta Tau Deltas. (Courtesy of Marge Conly.)

GIRLS STUNT DAY AT BUTLER, C. 1915. Members of Kappa Alpha Theta compete in the YWCA's annual Stunt Day, which was a talent/variety show that members of Butler's fraternity and sorority houses competed in with songs, skits, and acrobatic stunts. The Kappas performed "Jack in the Box," complete with clown outfits, most of which were handmade. (Courtesy of Marge Conly.)

KAPPA ALPHA THETA, 1923. The Kappa Alpha Theta sorority was known as the "American beauties" of the Irvington Butler campus. Located at 215 South Butler Avenue, the home was beautifully appointed with the latest styles and had a baby grand piano in the parlor. (Photograph by Frank Jones, courtesy of Butler University.)

LAMBDA CHI ALPHA, 1923. The Lambda Chi Alphas were an intellectual fraternity located at 24 South Butler Avenue, with the proud motto, "When do we eat?" Organized in 1909 in Boston, Lambda Chi Alpha is today one of the largest general male fraternities in America. (Photograph by Frank Jones, courtesy of Butler University.)

PHI DELTA THETA, 1923. Located at 5020 East Pleasant Run Parkway, North Drive, the Phi Delta Theta house used the line from Edgar Allan Poe's tome, "Quoth the raven," as their motto. The Phi Delta Thetas were founded in 1848 at the University of Miami in Oxford, Ohio. The first chapter of the fraternity was chartered at Indiana University in 1849, and the Butler chapter was chartered 10 years later. (Photograph by Frank Jones, courtesy of Butler University.)

PI BETA PHI, 1923. Following the motto "Take Notice," the ladies of this sorority, true to their sisterhood, pose on the porch of their house at 275 South Audubon Road. Beginning with 12 members at Monmouth College in 1867, this sorority continued a trend that began in the decade prior to the Civil War when women students, wanting to enjoy the same secret-society privileges that men had, adopted Greek letters for their own select social groups. (Photograph by Frank Jones, courtesy of Butler University.)

SIGMA CHI, 1923. Still a popular fraternity on the present-day Butler University campus, in the 1920s, Sigma Chi embodied "perfect harmony." Located at 209 South Downey Avenue just down the street from the Bona Thompson Memorial Library, Sigma Chi defined fraternity as "an obligation, a necessity, an introduction, a requirement, a passport, a lesson, an influence, an opportunity, an investment, a peacemaker and a pleasure." (Photograph by Frank Jones, courtesy of Butler University.)

DELTA DELTA DELTA, 1923. The Delta Delta Delta motto is to promote the ideals of truth, self-sacrifice, and friendship, and at 5621 Beechwood Avenue, one of the sorority's homes in Irvington, that is exactly what the girls did. The home was located near the famous Kile oak tree and the home of Lucille Morehouse, who was a valued art critic for the *Indianapolis Star*. (Photograph by Frank Jones, courtesy of Butler University.)

ZETA TAU ALPHA, 1923. Zeta Tau Alpha's "twenty angels" lived in a Queen Anne–style home at 69 North Irvington Avenue. Founded in Virginia in 1898, the original nine sisters were only 14 or 15 years of age. Using the motto "Seek the Noblest," the sorority still has a presence at Indiana University, Purdue University, Franklin College, Indiana State, and the University of Evansville. (Photograph by Frank Jones, courtesy of Butler University.)

KAPPA KAPPA GAMMA, 1923. One of the most famous sorority houses was the Kappa Kappa Gamma house located in the William H. H. Graham house at 5432 University Avenue. The home was built in 1889 and became the residence for many Greek houses during the Butler years in Irvington, including Phi Delta Theta and Chi Rho Zeta. (Photograph by Frank Jones, courtesy of Butler University.)

**KATHARINE MERRILL GRAYDON,
c. 1926.** Katharine Merrill Graydon was a professor of English language and literature at Butler College for many years. She lived at 303 South Downey Avenue and served as a mentor to many Butler graduates. However, Graydon was not without controversy. Rumors of a scandal involving Graydon and Indiana University president and assistant professor of Greek Dr. Lemuel Moss sparked the couple's hasty departure from Indiana University's Bloomington campus in 1884. Graydon went on to tutor naturalist John Muir's daughters and teach at Oahu College in Hawaii before coming to Butler in 1907. To legions of alumni she was the "spirit of Butler." These photographs were taken at a meeting of the Katharine Merrill Graydon Club in Kokomo with several Butler alumni. (Courtesy of Marge Conly.)

"COLLEGE OF MISSIONS" THE SARAH DAVIS DETERDING MEMORIAL. INDIANAPOLIS. IND.

THE COLLEGE OF MISSIONS. Although it was not a Butler College building, the College of Missions is considered by many to be part of the Butler campus. Operated by the Christian Women's Board of Missions, the tie to Butler was natural as the two schools often offered credit for each other's classes. The purpose of the College of Missions was to train Christian Church (Disciples of Christ) missionaries, who served within the United States and overseas. The cornerstone of the building was laid on August 10, 1907, but it was not completed for three years. The four-story structure offered a gymnasium, a science laboratory, and sewing and music rooms on the first floor, administrative offices and a chapel on the second floor, and classrooms and sleeping quarters on the third floor. The fourth floor housed the kitchen and additional dormitories. (Above, courtesy of Don and Lisa Flick; below, courtesy of Larry Muncie.)

MISSIONARIES OF IRVINGTON. Throughout its tenure in Irvington, the College of Missions sent its graduates to missions in Jamaica, India, Mexico, Puerto Rico, Argentina, and Paraguay. The missions offered outreach programs throughout the United States as well. Among the many notable Irvington missionaries were, from left to right, Nellie Huexander, C. N. Smiley, Helen McGarerau, and unidentified. (Courtesy of Irvington Historical Society Archives.)

COLLEGE OF MISSIONS FACULTY, 1922–1923. Faculty members from the latter days of the college included (first row) J. C. Garritt, Mrs. A. F. Hensey, G. W. Brown, Mrs. R. K. McClay, A. F. Hensey, and A. R. Miles; (second row) S. Kato, Dr. Hope Nichoson, J. H. Walker, Grace McGavran, Anna F. Weaver, and D. A. McGavran; (third row) O. J. Grainger, C. M. Morton, and Y. C. Lee. (Courtesy of Irvington Historical Society Archives.)

GRADUATION CEREMONY, COLLEGE OF MISSIONS. Graduates of the College of Missions receive blessings before participating in the annual ivy ring ceremony on the front lawn of the missions building. During the ceremony, ivy was taken from the walls of the building and held between graduates to form a symbolic chain during commencement exercises. Between the years 1910 and 1927, the College of Missions graduated 309 students. In 1928, after Butler University moved to the north side of Indianapolis, the College of Missions moved to Hartford, Connecticut, and later its library was moved to the divinity school at Yale University. (Courtesy of Irvington Historical Society Archives.)

THE DEMOLITION OF BUTLER, C. 1939. The relocation of Butler to its current Fairview campus was hard on the Irvington community, but when enrollment swelled after World War I, expansion became a necessity. Irvington residents pledged financial resources to keep Butler in the community, but when the school moved, the vacant buildings fell to vandalism and the effects of time before being systematically demolished. The community of Irvington did not stop supporting Butler, however. Many residents still attended the school on the north side of Indianapolis, and in the 1940s, the Irvington Women's Club turned over several bonds to the campus. (Courtesy of Larry Muncie.)

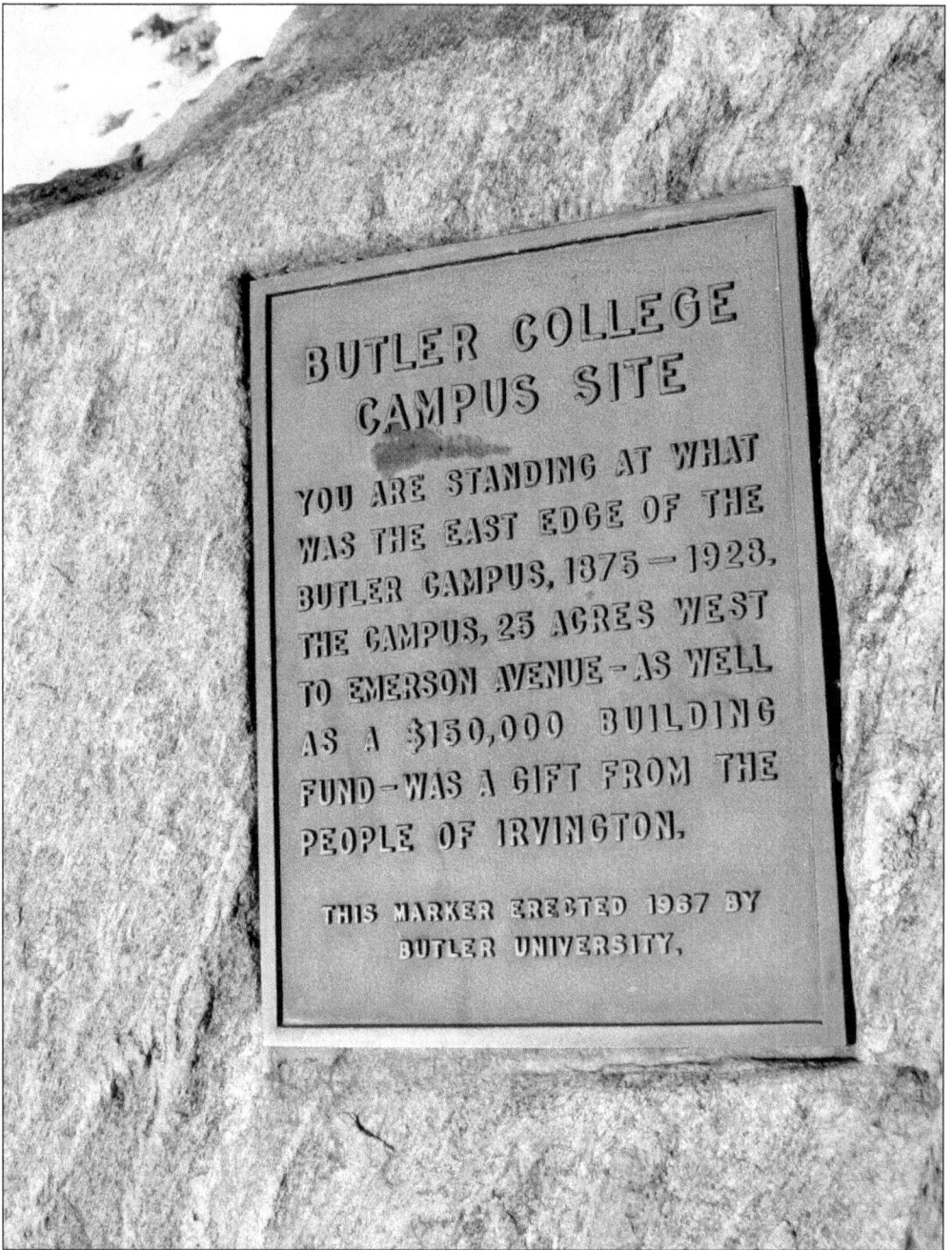

BUTLER COLLEGE COMMEMORATIVE PLAQUE. Today the old Butler campus has been replaced by homes and streets, but the spirit of the school lives on in the community. In 1967, a stone and plaque was placed by Butler University at the corner of University and Butler Avenues to commemorate Butler's years on the east side from 1875 to 1928 and in appreciation of the community for its donation of the land and initial financing. Other than the Bona Thompson Memorial Library and homes that served as residences for Butler students and faculty like the Benton House, only photographs and yellowed clippings remain from the Butler days in Irvington. (Author's collection.)

Three

A CORNUCOPIA OF DESIGN

As the early Irvington residents set about establishing their community, they wanted to create a place that reflected the area's diversity while keeping up with the style of the times. Nowhere is this more evident than in the neighborhood's architecture, which incorporates every design style from the 1870s to the 1950s. In fact, many of today's Irvington residents painstakingly research their abodes to keep them true to their individual time periods.

Early homes, such as Jacob Julian's Second Empire–style mansion boasted a lot of Romantic influences with elaborate detailing. Homes of this style and the Italianate style of architecture were popular in Irvington. One of the best-known surviving examples of a typical Victorian structure is the Benton House at 312 South Downey Avenue, which was the residence of Butler University president Allen R. Benton.

As the 20th century approached, there was an increase in the amount of lumber used for building as opposed to brick. The grand and elaborate homes gave way to Queen Anne–style cottage homes, which combined elaborate detailing and formal floor plans on a smaller scale. As the craftsman style became popular, the homes of the early 1900s offered homeowners more informal abodes with modern appointments setting them apart from their Victorian counterparts.

Bungalows eventually came onto the scene with traditional one-story floor plans and low-pitched roofs. Those residents who enjoyed a larger home often built Colonial Revival–period homes that were known for their symmetry and block-style exteriors similar to the Georgian and Federal houses that grace the East Coast. Many of these homes can be seen along Pleasant Run Parkway adjacent to Ellenberger Park. Another style of that period, Tudor Revival, can also be seen in homes throughout the Irvington area.

By the 1920s through the 1940s, there was more of a need for smaller homes in Irvington. In response to this need, "kit" homes sold by the Sears company, along with a variety of homes constructed by local builders, provided Irvington with housing options to fit nearly every taste and budget.

JULIAN-LAYMAN HOUSE. This Victorian mansion was built by Irvington cofounder Jacob Julian and was one of the earliest homes in Irvington. The house sat on a spacious lot on Audubon Road, which is now the site of the Saxony Apartments. The home helped establish the Second Empire style as the representative design for other homes to be built in the town. Indianapolis merchant James T. Layman and his family lived in this home until the early 1950s. (Courtesy of Larry Muncie.)

GEORGE W. JULIAN HOME. Still standing today, the George W. Julian home is located at 115 South Audubon Road. Julian, a former member of Congress and an abolitionist, was the brother of Jacob Julian. After George's death, his daughter Grace Julian Clarke, a noted women's rights leader, continued to live in the Italianate-style house. It subsequently became a boardinghouse and a sanitarium. Today the home is again a private residence that has been painstakingly restored. (Courtesy of Irvington Historical Society Archives.)

EUDORUS JOHNSON HOME. Truly steeped in Victorian Gothic architecture, the Eudorus "Dora" Johnson home on the southwest corner of Audubon Road and University Avenue opposite Irving Circle was built in 1876 and features round turrets, high gables, and a steeple roof. Johnson was the son of Sylvester Johnson and served as deputy auditor and deputy treasurer of Marion County for several years. He also was Indianapolis city controller in the late 1890s and spent his years after public service in the banking sector until his death in 1908. (Courtesy of Irvington Historical Society Archives.)

BELZER HOUSE. Of the many Queen Anne–style homes in Irvington, the Belzer house at 320 South Audubon Road is an unusual design plan that uses contrasting masses as opposed to texture to create the overall feel of the style. The home was owned by Francis "Chief" Belzer, who taught shop at school 57 and who led the Indianapolis and Central Indiana Boy Scout Council for many years. (Author's collection.)

THE BENTON HOUSE. Probably one of the most famous homes in Irvington is the Benton house. Built in 1873 by Nicholas Ohmer, the Benton house at 312 South Downey Avenue is an example of Second Empire style. The home was considered to be a "spec" home in Irvington to give prospective homeowners an example of what their houses could look like. A rental for several years, the house was home to noted evangelist Louise Robinson, who helped organize the Irvington United Methodist Church. It was purchased by the Fredrick Kautz family in 1888, although they never lived there. The home was eventually sold to Dr. Allen R. Benton, who was president of Butler University from 1886 to 1891. Benton made several modifications to the home, which local historians believe to be the upper rooms of the rear portion of the house. The illustration below was drawn by Don Dick. (Above, author's collection; below, courtesy of Bea Cottom.)

THE BENTON HOUSE, INTERIOR.
The Benton house is a museum home filled with many antiques and is on the National Register of Historic Places. The home is the meeting place for several Irvington organizations, including the Benton House Association, and was completely restored by the Irvington Historic Landmarks Foundation in 1966. Dr. Allen R. Benton lived in the house nearly 20 years. His wife, Silence, died in 1900, and Benton remained in the house until 1907, when he retired and returned to Lincoln, Nebraska. He died on January 1, 1914. (Photographs by K. C. Leffler, courtesy of Irvington Historical Society.)

KIN HUBBARD'S HOME, POSTCARD. In 1909, Frank Hunter, a well-known Indianapolis architect, was asked to design a bungalow-style home for Frank McKinney "Kin" Hubbard, the creator of "Abe Martin." The home was located high on a hill at New York Street and Emerson Avenue overlooking Pleasant Run Parkway and across the creek from another Hunter-designed structure, the Phi Delta Theta fraternity house. The lot was sold to Hubbard by another prominent Irvington resident, Hilton U. Brown. (Courtesy of Larry Muncie.)

FORREST-CARR HOUSE. The Jacob Dorsey Forrest home at 30 North Audubon Road on Audubon Circle is an example of a Tudor Revival–style home. It was built in 1906, and Thomas Carr Howe purchased the home in 1914 when he was president of Butler College. Howe sold the home to the Irvington United Methodist Church in 1924. (Courtesy of Irvington United Methodist Church.)

WILLIAM FORSYTH HOME. Indiana artist William Forsyth's home and studio was located at 15 South Emerson Avenue. He lived there from 1906 until his death in 1935. His daughter Constance was also a painter. According to Marge Conly, a relative of Forsyth's, "cousin Will" did not like a lot of children in his studio. The home and studio have been razed. (Courtesy of Irvington Historical Society Archives.)

ROBERTSON HOME. The house at 65 North Ritter Avenue was built by Louis A. Robertson and his brother for their parents, David and Orinthia Robertson. The couple celebrated their 50th wedding anniversary in the parlor of the home in 1911. Eventually, their son Frank, who was a doctor, lived and had his practice in the home until he died in 1925. (Courtesy of Mark and Cathy Kippert.)

WILLIAM THOMAS MCVEY HOME. William Thomas McVey built the home at 211 Good Avenue for $900 after purchasing the lot for $25. The home, which was the first one built on the street, is comprised of materials salvaged from some of his other projects that included Butler faculty homes along Downey Avenue. (Courtesy of Lori Malander.)

DISSETTE PROPERTY. Located on the present site of Pleasant Run Golf Course, the Dissette property was a big draw for local children. Some are shown here playing on a bridge located on the property. The property was owned by James Dissette, the founder of American National Bank, who built his home on the site in 1909. (Courtesy of Larry Muncie.)

HIBBEN HOUSE. Thomas Hibben Sr. bought this house, which had previously been the home of the James Downey and Edward Thompson families. Located on the southeast corner of Downey and University Avenues, Hibben had the house altered and the grounds landscaped. Hibben's daughter Helene, a sculptor, started her private children's school in this house. Hibben's son Thomas Jr., an architect, specialized in the arts and crafts movement. (Courtesy of Larry Muncie.)

FOURTH OF JULY. Theodore Portteus can be seen standing outside his one-and-a-half-story Queen Anne–style home at 306 North Irvington Avenue in this 1916 photograph. Portteus served as the sheriff of Marion County in the early 1900s and owned a dry goods store along Washington Street. He not only helped facilitate Irvington's annexation but as an Indianapolis city councilor he is also credited for renaming many of the Irvington streets once the town became part of the city. (Courtesy of Larry Muncie.)

H. H. Holmes Rental Site. When Dr. H. H. Holmes, using the alias Dr. A. E. Cook, rented a home at this site near Bolton and Julian Avenues, no one in the Irvington community could have known that they were playing host to America's first serial killer. After murdering more than 200 people in the "Holmes murder castle" during the Chicago World's Fair, Holmes created an insurance fraud scheme with an associate, Benjamin Pitezel, in which the two planned to fake Pitezel's death and split the insurance proceeds. Holmes ultimately murdered Pitezel and kidnapped the man's three children—two daughters and a son, Howard. The two girls were killed in Toronto, Canada, and then Holmes relocated to Irvington where he rented a home of similar design and promptly installed a commercial-grade wood-burning stove. When Holmes was eventually arrested for Pitezel's murder, investigators followed Holmes's tracks to Irvington, where they found the remains of the 10-year-old boy. Holmes only confessed to 27 murders, but it was enough to convict and hang him publicly in Philadelphia on May 7, 1896. (Author's collection.)

THE BUNGALOW BOOM. Bungalow-style houses offered homeowners the opportunity to have a place that was a little more modern than their early Irvington counterparts. Many of these homes are located along Pleasant Run Parkway and feature less detailing, although stucco was a popular embellishment and a more elongated roofline was common. The Harder home, pictured in 1913, was located at 115 South Emerson Avenue. (Courtesy of Irvington Historical Society Archives.)

JOHN MAHONEY'S HOME, 1932. The Mahoney home was one of the first houses built on Ritter Avenue near Tenth Street before the area was developed. It was built by John Mahoney and his wife, Minnie, and it still stands today. He was a photographer in the area. (Courtesy of Judith Nichols.)

THE KINCAID HOUSE, 1908. Martha May Kincaid stands outside her home at 51 South Ritter Avenue on the corner of Julian Avenue. The home was built in 1881 and was one of the earliest stick-style homes in the neighborhood. (Courtesy of Larry Muncie.)

WILLIAM KAESER RESIDENCE. William Kaeser came to the United States in 1923 and attended art school in New York City. Eventually he graduated from the John Herron Art School in Indianapolis. He studied under William Forsyth and was a member of the Irvington group of artists. He lived not only at this 316 South Audubon Road address but also at 333 South Emerson Avenue where he had both a home and studio. (Author's collection.)

SIGMA CHI HOUSE. Throughout the Irvington neighborhood, there are many homes that were used as fraternity and sorority houses by Butler College students. This house at 209 South Downey Avenue was the home to the Sigma Chi fraternity. It is one of the many Queen Anne–style homes of the neighborhood that remain today. (Author's collection.)

KATHARINE MERRILL GRAYDON'S HOME. Built in 1908 by Foltz and Parker architects, the home of Butler faculty member Katharine Merrill Graydon was part of the arts and crafts–style that peppers the Irvington landscape. The architectural company not only designed this home for Graydon but it was also responsible for the design of school 57, the Marion County Children's Guardians Home, and other Irvington buildings. (Author's collection.)

INGELSIDE. Although no one knows who the architect was for this Victorian Gothic home located at 359 South Ritter Avenue, the name Ingelside reflects its first owner, Mrs. Ingel, who ran a boardinghouse for women attending Butler University. According to Hilton U. Brown, "half of the college [romances] in the first five years after [Butler] came to Irvington may be safely credited to this place." (Author's collection.)

ELIJAH JOHNSON HOME. A perfect example of a hybrid-style home is the Queen Anne–arts and crafts home of Dr. Elijah and Martha Johnson at 304 South Downey Avenue. The home features flared wood shingle-sided walls and a bell-cast, clipped gable roof. Johnson lived in the home from 1909 to 1945. He was a professor of mathematics at Butler and served as the treasurer for the university from 1924 to 1929. (Author's collection.)

KAPPA KAPPA GAMMA HOUSE. Over the years, this sorority was located in several houses throughout Irvington, including this one at 236 South Ritter Avenue. The sorority was founded at Monmouth College in Monmouth, Illinois, in 1870, and the Butler chapter was established on January 2, 1878. The sorority occupied the home in the above picture from 1927 to 1928 after vacating a previous residence at 254 South Ritter Avenue in 1919. (Author's collection.)

D. C. STEPHENSON MANSION. After William H. H. Graham died, Mrs. Graham continued to live in the house at 5432 University Avenue until the early 1920s, when it was sold to David Curtis (D. C.) Stephenson. Stephenson spent $20,000 renovating the house, including adding the pillared portico, giving the home the look of a southern plantation mansion. Stephenson, who was the grand dragon of the Ku Klux Klan, wanted the home to resemble Klankrest, the Klan's Atlanta, Georgia, headquarters. (Courtesy of Irvington Historical Society Archives.)

MADGE OBERHOLTZER HOME. Just as the David Curtis (D. C.) Stephenson mansion is an infamous landmark in Irvington, the Oberholtzer home at 5802 University Avenue also became noted after the death of its resident Madge Oberholtzer. The home was built in 1909 and was sold in 1916 to George Oberholtzer, who was an inspector for the U.S. Railway Mail Service and vice president of the U.S. Railway Mail Clerk's Association. Madge, a former Butler College student, was a statehouse secretary when she met D. C. Stephenson, who often made advances on young women. She saw Stephenson socially on occasion and repeatedly turned down his advances. Stephenson devised other measures to get her to bend to his will, which resulted in her death at this home in 1925. (Author's collection.)

Four

IRVINGTON

CONGREGATIONS

Although founded on the beliefs and tenants of Quaker visionaries, Irvington quickly became a varied religious community. No matter what a person's faith might be, there seemed to be a religious affiliation to meet those spiritual needs.

Irvington's first religious organization was the Downey Avenue Christian Church, which found among its members many of Butler University's earliest faculty and other prominent Irvington residents, including Hilton U. Brown. Founded in 1878, the Irvington United Methodist Church was another early congregation and is home to Troop 9, one of the oldest Boy Scout troops in the city. The front portion of the church that stands on Audubon Circle is the former residence of Thomas Carr Howe, Butler president and namesake of T. C. Howe Academy. The first church with a large African American congregation, Irvington First Baptist began in 1887.

By the start of the 20th century, many other churches joined the ranks of Irvington's spiritual offerings. Irvington Presbyterian on Johnson Avenue is one of the largest Irvington church structures and has gained some notoriety as the place where the first Girl Scout troop in Indianapolis was organized. It is said that Butler College played a big role in getting the Presbyterian Church started in Irvington by helping with the initial building fund. Our Lady of Lourdes became the town's Roman Catholic parish and today boasts a healthy membership, not only in its congregation but also in the adjoining parochial school.

Throughout the year, the Irvington congregations work together for the benefit of the entire community through rummage sales, fish fries, festivals, and pitching in on large-scale neighborhood events, such as the community Thanksgiving dinner, the luminaria at Christmas, Celebrate Irvington in the spring, and the legendary Halloween festival in the fall.

From humble beginnings, many of which were started in log cabins or other simple structures, to the stately edifices erected over time, Irvington's church architecture ranges from the traditional to modern, offering an attractive balance. While buildings have changed and members have come and gone, there remains the steadfast presence of several congregations within the east-side town.

DOWNEY AVENUE CHRISTIAN CHURCH. The oldest congregation in Irvington was founded in 1875 with 40 members on the register. For many years, church services were held in the main building of Butler University, where a number of members were faculty or staff at the university. Otis Burgess was not only the president of the school but also a minister for the church. These photographs show two views of the original church building, made of red brick on the corner of Julian and Downey Avenues, which was dedicated in 1893. (Courtesy of Downey Avenue Christian Church.)

MEN'S BIBLE CLASS, C. 1913. Before the three-story education wing made from Indiana limestone was added in 1914, the men of Downey Avenue Christian Church gathered in this wooden structure to hold their Bible classes. This group includes some of the most prominent names in Irvington during the Edwardian era, including Hilton U. Brown, Scot Butler, and Thomas Carr Howe. (Courtesy of Downey Avenue Christian Church.)

WILLING WORKERS SUNDAY SCHOOL CLASS, 1912. Standing in front of the old church, the women who comprised Downey Avenue Christian's congregation and the Disciples of Christ ministry were not only important to the town of Irvington but also to the College of Missions by helping to raise the needed $100,000 to construct the Mission's building. (Courtesy of Downey Avenue Christian Church.)

GROUND BREAKING FOR THE NEW CHURCH, 1950. In 1950, Downey Avenue Christian Church was ready to expand once again, and church leaders began a fund drive for the needed $75,000 it would take to build the new sanctuary. Thanks to generous donations by congregation members, the goal was quickly met, and designs were drawn by Edward J. Clark, the architect for the new building. (Courtesy of Downey Avenue Christian Church.)

DOWNEY AVENUE CHRISTIAN CHURCH, C. 1953. The cornerstone for the new church was laid in 1952, and the first services in the new building were held in November 1953. The exterior was constructed from stone and has a more modern look than its predecessor. The new education wing was constructed in 1962 and today is home to a cooperative preschool during the week. (Courtesy of Downey Avenue Christian Church.)

64

ELEANOR PUTNAM. Eleanor Putnam, the wife of James W., was a member of Downey Avenue Christian Church and is credited with founding of the first troop of Campfire Girls in the city of Indianapolis. Campfire Girls was founded in 1910 as the first nonsectarian, interracial organization for girls in the United States. Boys were admitted starting in 1975. (Courtesy of Downey Avenue Christian Church.)

DOWNEY AVENUE YOUTH MINISTRIES. The youth of the Downey Avenue Christian congregation were always encouraged to become involved and to be active members within the church. Parents often organized a variety of dances and wholesome club activities for the younger generation to participate in. These two boys are on their way to Bible study class around 1954. (Courtesy of Downey Avenue Christian Church.)

MANY HOUSES OF IRVINGTON UNITED METHODIST CHURCH. The Irvington United Methodist Church has been a staple in the community whether it was in a log cabin or in the Layman Avenue church or on the circle at 30 North Audubon Road. These drawings for the church's 75th anniversary show the various buildings that housed Irvington's second-oldest congregation over the years. (Courtesy of Irvington United Methodist Church.)

NEW SANCTUARY GROUND BREAKING. The ground breaking for the new Irvington Methodist Episcopal Church was held in May 1925. In this photograph, the entire congregation came out to support the planned structure, designed by architect Herbert Foltz. The building cost $218,574. It was dedicated on September 12, 1926. (Courtesy of Irvington United Methodist Church.)

IRVINGTON UNITED METHODIST CHURCH, TWO VIEWS. Located at the center of Audubon Circle and attached to the home once owned by J. D. Forrest and Thomas Carr Howe, the Irvington United Methodist Church was first organized in 1878 as the Methodist Episcopal Church. Originally housed in an old township school, the church had structures at two other sites before building at its current location. Lou Robertson suggested the location on the circle when it was decided that the church should be moved from Layman Avenue. Howe was agreeable to selling the property and gave a speech at the dedication ceremony on September 12, 1926, with 1,000 congregants present. (Courtesy of Irvington United Methodist Church.)

BOY SCOUT TROOP 9. This photograph of Boy Scout Troop 9 shows Aston Wood, Robert Merkle, Forrest Morgan, Donald Curry, Gerald Shortridge, Norman Shortridge, Robert Fitzgerald, Ralph Cook, Charles James, Willis Overly, Grant Judd, Guff Servis, William Kiser, Leslie Smith, Chester Barney, Greer Shotwell, Ralph Ellidge, Thomas Harrison, John Wamsley, Stanley Ryker, William Harrison, Noble Ropkey, Herbert Stewart, and C. C. Osborne. (Courtesy of Irvington Historical Society Archives.)

CONSTRUCTION OF NEW EDUCATION WING. This photograph shows the construction on the west side of the original building that eventually became the education wing of Irvington United Methodist church with various classrooms for Bible study and Sunday school classes. Today the education wing is home to the church's preschool. (Courtesy of Irvington United Methodist Church.)

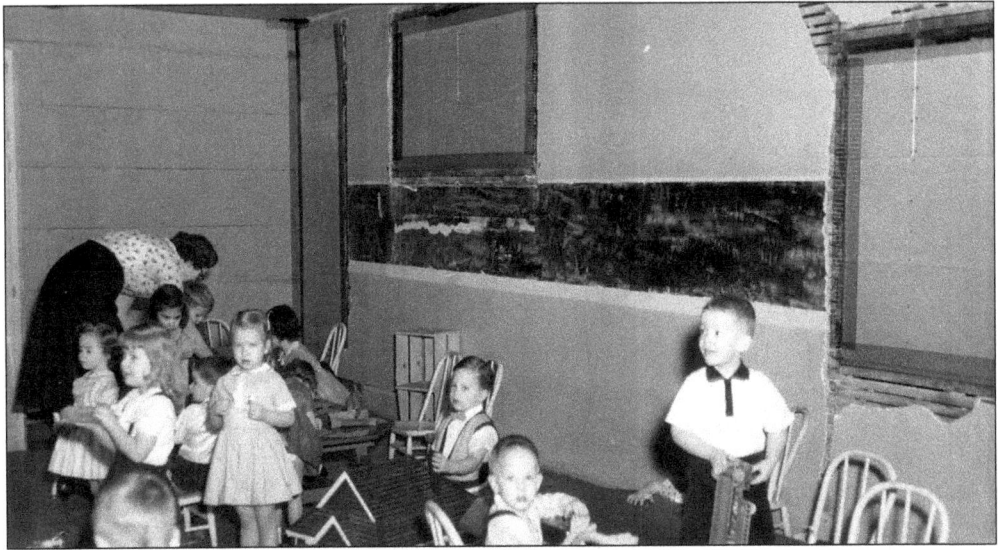

Two Irvington United Methodist Church Classrooms. These two photographs show the difference a little renovation can make. Above, plaster and other debris can be seen in this classroom that is under construction around 1958. The church was being renovated with the addition of a new wing. Below, the finished product, a gleaming, shiny, new classroom, is ready for preschoolers. Architects Garnes and Moore designed not only the classrooms but also the remodeling of the youth center, parlor, and construction of a chapel. The remodeling of the main sanctuary began in 1963 with dedication services held in October. (Courtesy of Irvington United Methodist Church.)

SUNDAY SCHOOL CLASSES, 1906. From the size of these boys' and girls' Sunday school classes, it is easy to see how large the Irvington Presbyterian Church congregation was. Space, as with other churches in the Irvington neighborhood, was becoming an issue. Although a gymnasium was added in the 1920s, the congregation was still growing and the gymnasium did not provide adequate room. It was obvious that a new church building was needed. By 1924, plans were in motion for a new structure that would provide enough room for the expanding congregation. (Courtesy of Irvington Presbyterian Church.)

EARLY SCOUT PICNIC, C. 1913. Irvington Presbyterian Church was known for its influence in the Scouting movement. Home to the first Girl Scout troop in the city of Indianapolis and subsequently holding one of the first cookie sales to help finance Scout camp, the congregation was involved in the Boy Scouts of America as well. (Courtesy of Irvington Presbyterian Church.)

SUNDAY SCHOOL CLASS, 1910. A group of youths from Irvington Presbyterian Church pose for a picture. The inclusion of the rifle, rope, and knife suggest that the youngsters might have been part of a Boy Scout troop as well. Pictured from left to right are (first row) Bud Bunnell, Walter Porter, and Clyde McVey; (second row) John Wamsley, Walter McCoy, Albert Stone, Harold Wilson, and Ray Woods. (Courtesy of Irvington Presbyterian Church.)

LAYING OF THE CORNERSTONE, IRVINGTON PRESBYTERIAN CHURCH, 1929. Rev. Jonathan Day gave the dedication address to members who attended the ceremony on March 10, 1929. The church was to be a Gothic structure and made of Bedford limestone with dark oak and hammer beam ceiling trusses. According to church history, there was a controversy surrounding whether or not the bell from the original church should hang in the new building. Although the bell was initially jettisoned, it was found sometime later in a coal yard, restored, and hung in the church's bell tower by 1931. (Courtesy of Irvington Presbyterian Church.)

IRVINGTON PRESBYTERIAN CHURCH, c. 1950. The current building was constructed in 1929 with Tudor Gothic influences throughout. Architects Harrison and Turnock, who were responsible for the design of the building, wanted an edifice worthy of the solemn events that would take place there. The result was so impressive that the church design was honored by the National Association of Architects in 1929 for its quality. Over the years, the church has seen many renovations, remains one of the most impressive churches in Irvington, and boasts a very active congregation. (Courtesy of Irvington Presbyterian Church.)

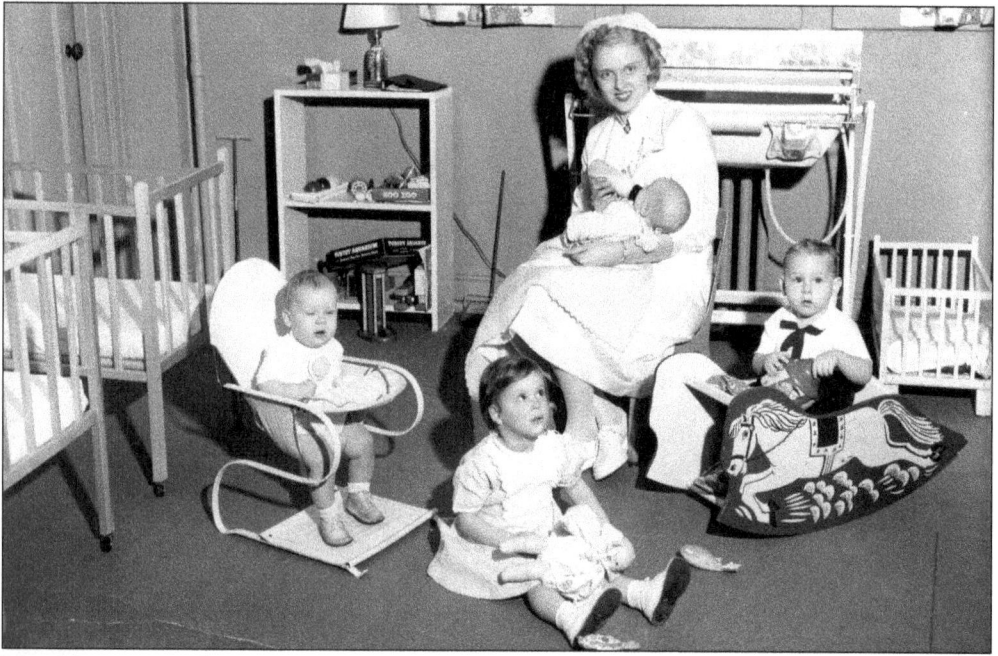

NEW NURSERY AT IRVINGTON PRESBYTERIAN CHURCH, C. 1955. Mrs. Robert Eddy poses with some of Irvington Presbyterian Church's youngest members in the crib room as their parents attend Sunday services. Throughout the 1950s, Irvington Presbyterian was remodeled several times. The gymnasium was converted into classrooms and meeting areas, and a youth parlor was added. (Courtesy of Irvington Presbyterian Church.)

VACATION BIBLE SCHOOL KICKBALL GAME, C. 1955. Irvington Presbyterian Church initiated its vacation Bible school program in 1923, reaching out to the other churches in the community to form a united program. It only lasted two years before Irvington Presbyterian Church assumed the responsibility for the program and welcomed all children from throughout the community. The program included music, games, crafts, and religious education. (Courtesy of Irvington Presbyterian Church.)

OUR LADY OF LOURDES ORIGINAL BUILDING. Irvington's Roman Catholic parish, Our Lady of Lourdes, was founded in 1909 at 5317 East Washington Street. The property was purchased for $2,600, and Fr. Joseph Poelhuis was appointed the first pastor of the new parish. Built in 1915, this building was used for worship and school purposes until the present church building was completed in 1942. It then continued to serve as the parish school building until 1958. (Courtesy of Our Lady of Lourdes Catholic Church.)

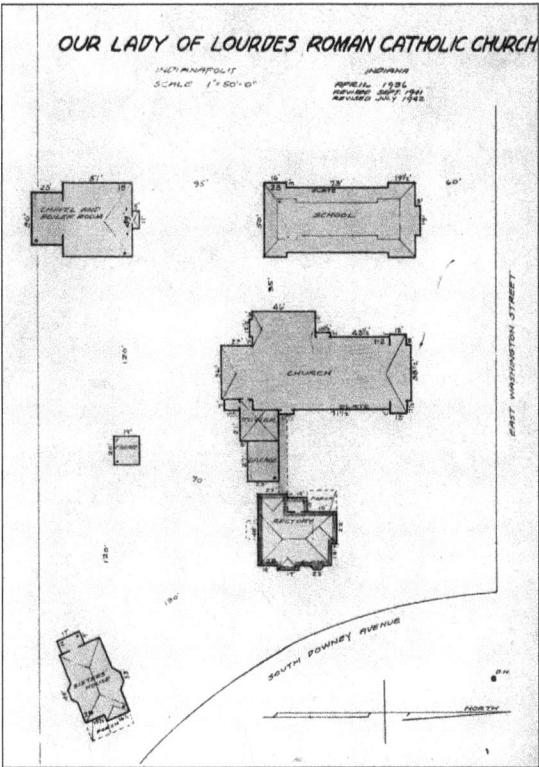

OUR LADY OF LOURDES PROPERTY. This map shows the layout of the Our Lady of Lourdes campus in 1946. In 1911, the Parker family property in Irvington was purchased in order to create room for the expanding parish. By 1915, members included 200 families, which created a need for the school building and a convent for the Sisters of St. Francis who taught at the school. (Courtesy of Our Lady of Lourdes Catholic Church.)

75

MSGR. MICHAEL LYONS. Fr. Michael Lyons became the second pastor of Our Lady of Lourdes Church, taking over from Fr. Joseph Poelhuis in 1919. One of his first acts as pastor was to reorganize the men's club of the church. By 1925, the parish had grown rapidly, and there was a consensus that something needed to be done to alleviate the overcrowding of the church, as at least 200 parishioners from Lourdes were reassigned to nearby Little Flower. He authorized the building of Bernadette Hall as an auxiliary church building. As the parish continued to grow, Lyons was elevated to the rank of monsignor on December 6, 1938. He resigned from his post on October 6, 1940, but remained in the parish as pastor emeritus. (Courtesy of Our Lady of Lourdes Catholic Church.)

FIRST COMMUNION MASS. Although it was about a month before the church was dedicated, there were several celebrations that preceded the solemn event, including a baptism and several weddings and funerals. The first mass in the new church building was held on May 24, 1942, to celebrate the first communion of 46 children. These photographs show a first communion processional from the front of the church building facing East Washington Street. Note the sign for the Moore and Kirk Funeral Home on the north side of the street, a business still at that location today. (Photographs by Donald J. Carr, courtesy of Our Lady of Lourdes Catholic Church.)

OUR LADY OF LOURDES NEW CHURCH, 1949. By 1940, plans were underway for a new church to accommodate the ever-growing parish. Fr. James Moore spearheaded this project with the cornerstone being laid in 1941. The dedication of the new church was held on June 21, 1942. (Courtesy of Our Lady of Lourdes Catholic Church.)

INTERIOR OUR LADY OF LOURDES, 1942. The interior of Our Lady of Lourdes Catholic Church features a Tudor Gothic style with pillars that resemble a medieval cathedral. This photograph was taken from the balcony during the solemn dedication ceremony on June 21, 1942. (Courtesy of Our Lady of Lourdes Catholic Church.)

OUR LADY OF LOURDES CONVENT. The Sisters of St. Francis-Oldenburg were instrumental in the education of many young Catholic children on the east side. This photograph shows the convent for the sisters adjacent to the school building. It has since been razed to make way for a new parish center and preschool building. (Courtesy of Our Lady of Lourdes Catholic Church.)

SISTERS OF ST. FRANCIS HOUSEWARMING PARTY. From left to right, Sisters Mary Paul Nett, Mary Paul Larson, Mary Inez Schuman, Katherine Paul, and Clare Marie Bosler open their housewarming presents after the convent renovation. The Sisters of St. Francis held a housewarming open house to allow the parishioners to see their new living quarters. (Courtesy of Our Lady of Lourdes Catholic Church.)

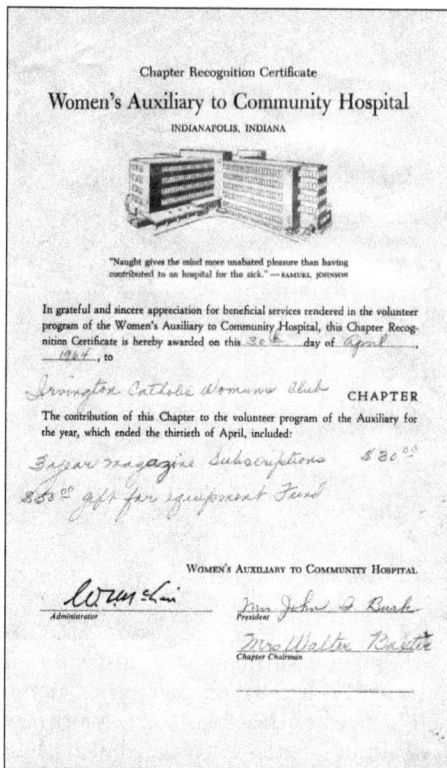

CITATION FOR COMMUNITY HOSPITAL AUXILIARY, 1964. This citation was given to the Irvington Catholic Women's Club on April 30, 1964, in recognition of its contributions to the hospital. What began as a small guild of first-grade mothers grew to include many members of the Our Lady of Lourdes parish. (Courtesy of Our Lady of Lourdes Catholic Church.)

FOURTH CHURCH OF CHRIST SCIENCE. In March 1922, the Fourth Church of Christ Science began its meetings in the Odd Fellows hall in Irvington with 96 members. Within months, the church was recognized by the national organization, but the church building on Pleasant Run Parkway was not dedicated until 1945. Because of declining membership, today the church is located on Audubon Road in a former shopping center. (Courtesy of Irvington Historical Society Archives.)

Five

INSIDE THE CLASSROOM

In spite of its primitive beginnings, the Irvington public school system ultimately flourished with a variety of learning institutions developing within the community from the Indianapolis Public School system to religious education. The George Washington Julian School 57 was the third public school building after the first two schoolhouses burned. Plans for the school were drawn in 1903 by Herbert Foltz. The school is located on the site of Dr. Levi Ritter's home at Washington Street and Ritter Avenue. To accommodate a growing student population, additions were made and portable classrooms were a common sight. Other public schools were built to meet Irvington's educational needs. These included school 58; George B. Loomis School 85, which is currently used as an office building; and school 77, located on Pleasant Run Parkway, which remained an Indianapolis Public School facility until 1980 when it became a private school. Today it is the site of the Irvington Community High School, a charter school.

Our Lady of Lourdes Church answered the need for parochial education when its first school opened in 1911 with the Sisters of St. Francis as primary educators. The original school was housed in the same structure as the church before the present school building was erected in 1958.

In 1938, Irvington constructed its first high school, Thomas Carr Howe High School, named after the former Butler president and prominent citizen of the community. The building was completed in 1939, and the school remained open until 1995 when it was closed only to reopen five years later as an Indianapolis Public Schools academy.

The people of Irvington believe in offering their residents a wealth of educational opportunities, and with the opening of the Irvington Community High School, a charter school option for both elementary and high school students, the neighborhood remains true to the vision of its founders that Irvington should be a place where education and academics are encouraged.

GEORGE W. JULIAN SCHOOL 57. Located at the corner of Washington Street and Ritter Avenue on the site of Dr. Levi Ritter's home, planning for the school began in 1903. For years, the building was simply known as the Irvington School until it was officially named for the former congressman and civil rights leader in 1930. (Courtesy of Don and Lisa Flick.)

THE JULIAN JOURNAL. George W. Julian School 57's newspaper announced important events like a visit from Sergeant Magnheimer and call for new crossing guards. Each paper sold for 3¢ and was complied by students and staff. (Courtesy of Howard Caldwell Jr.)

SCHOOL 57 REPORT CARD. Howard Caldwell's 1939 report card from school 57 showed that his best subjects were physical education, math, and music. The seventh grader passed the first semester of the year and was promoted to grade 7A for the following semester. Helen Loeper was the principal of the school at the time. (Courtesy of Howard Caldwell Jr.)

Indianapolis Public Schools
REPORT CARD
THE JUNIOR HIGH SCHOOL DIVISION
GRADES VII and VIII

Pupil's Name *Howard Caldwell*

Address *813 Hawthorne Lane* Phone *Ir. 0423*

School *57* Grade *7B*

Semester Ending *Jan. 20*, 193*9*

Home Room Teacher *Charlotte Sikes*

Principal *Helen Loeper*

SIGNATURE OF PARENT
Please acknowledge the receipt of this report card by signing your name as indicated below and return to the school at once. The third time the card is brought home it may be retained.

First Report *Mrs. H. C. Caldwell*
Parent, Signature

Second Report *Mrs. H. C. Caldwell*
Parent Signature

Assigned to Grade *7A* for next semester.

Principal *Helen Loeper*

NOTE TO PARENTS
The educational success of your child depends in a large measure upon the co-operation of the school and the home. You are cordially invited to visit the school to confer with the teacher and the principal concerning the progress of your child.
DeWITT S. MORGAN,
Superintendent of Schools.

SCHOOL 57 GRADUATING CLASS, 1930. A Depression-era 8A class assembled on the front steps of school 57 for its graduation picture. Irvington schools boasted high attendance rates, which led to the building of several other elementary schools in the area. Because of the need for educational facilities, students were often taught in portable classrooms on site and enrollment was sometimes limited. (Courtesy of Irvington Historical Society Archives.)

SCHOOL 57 STUDENTS. A group of students pose for a class photograph on the lawn of school 57 around 1929. Today the school is implementing a new curriculum and is taking steps to modernize a building that has remained true to its original concept. (Courtesy of Marge Conly.)

PAPER DRIVE, C. 1940S. During World War II, children were told that it was their patriotic duty to collect tin, paper, and other recyclable items to be reused for various needs. Boy Scout troops and others joined in the war effort, as shown by this paper drive at school 57, which literally took over the lawn of the school. (Courtesy of Irvington Historical Society Archives.)

SCHOOL SAFETY PATROL PARADE, 1927. This parade honoring school 57's safety record and the school's safety patrol gave children an opportunity to march down Washington Street along with civic groups and organizations. The number of children marching shows how many students were enrolled in the Irvington schools at the time. The importance of safety while walking to and from school was promoted across the city by the *Indianapolis News*. Children waved flags and made festive hats for the occasion. The sign on the truck below notes that there were 100 members of the school safety patrol at the time. (Courtesy of Irvington Historical Society Archives.)

THE HIBBEN SCHOOL. Helene Hibben opened a kindergarten in her Irvington home that was known for its costumed programs held throughout the year. This undated photograph shows a group of Irvington children getting ready for a performance. (Courtesy of Irvington Historical Society Archives.)

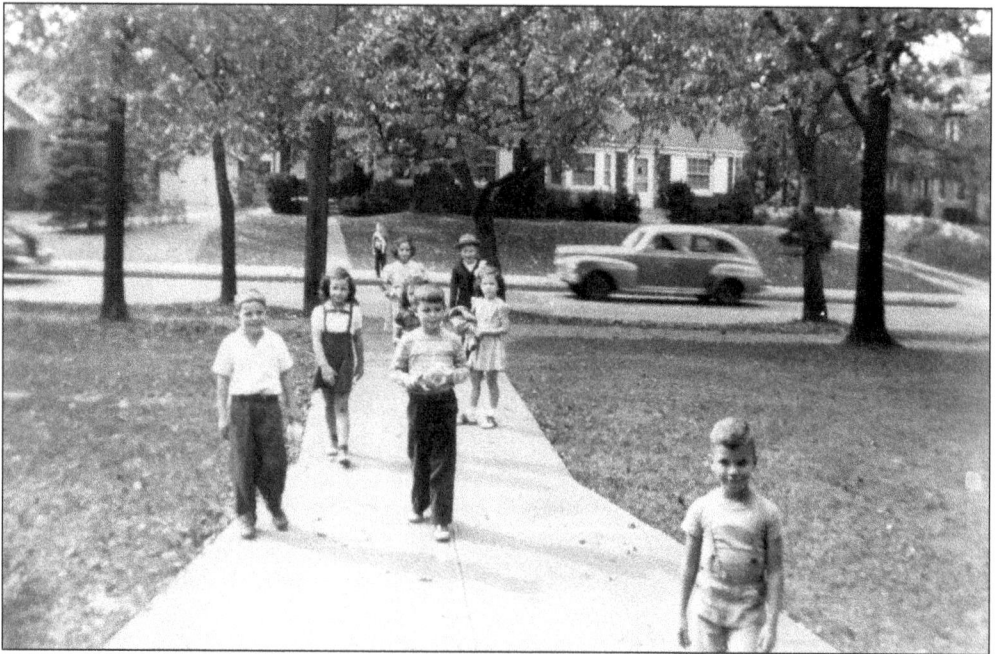

ARRIVAL AT SCHOOL 77, C. 1940. In the absence of buses, many Irvington children walked to school each day with the help of the school crossing guard (visible in the distance). These students are arriving for another busy day inside school 77, a portable school on North Arlington Avenue that served students living in northeast Irvington. (Courtesy of Larry Muncie.)

86

PUBLIC SCHOOL 77. School 77 began its long history at Pleasant Run Parkway and North Arlington Avenue in 1932 when portable classrooms that had been used to ease the overcrowding at school 82 while the new Christian Park School was built were moved from South Irvington to help alleviate the overcrowding at school 57. These photographs show the exterior of the building and the students participating in the morning flag-raising exercise. Twenty years later, the temporary school was demolished to make way for the modern public school building that was opened in 1952. The new school 77 was a concrete and brick structure. It served Irvington children until 1980 when the Indianapolis Public Schools closed the facility and it was purchased by a private school. Today the building is home to the Irvington Community High School, a charter school. (Courtesy of Larry Muncie.)

INDIANAPOLIS PUBLIC SCHOOL 85. Named for George B. Loomis, an accomplished music teacher and author of music textbooks for the Indianapolis Public School system, school 85, located on South Arlington Avenue, served families living between both sets of railroad tracks. Engineered by C. H. Ammerman and built by contractor William Jungclaus, the school opened in 1928 with two additional classrooms opening in 1930. Above is an illustration of school 85 by Thomas Stirling, former principal of Thomas Carr Howe High School. Below is a photograph of those students who were never tardy during the academic year standing in front of the school building. (Courtesy of Irvington Historical Society Archives.)

SCHOOL 85 BAND AND CORPS. This photograph from the early days of school 85 shows the fifth- and sixth-grade boys with their band instruments on June 8, 1928, possibly getting ready for a Flag Day performance. (Courtesy of Irvington Historical Society Archives.)

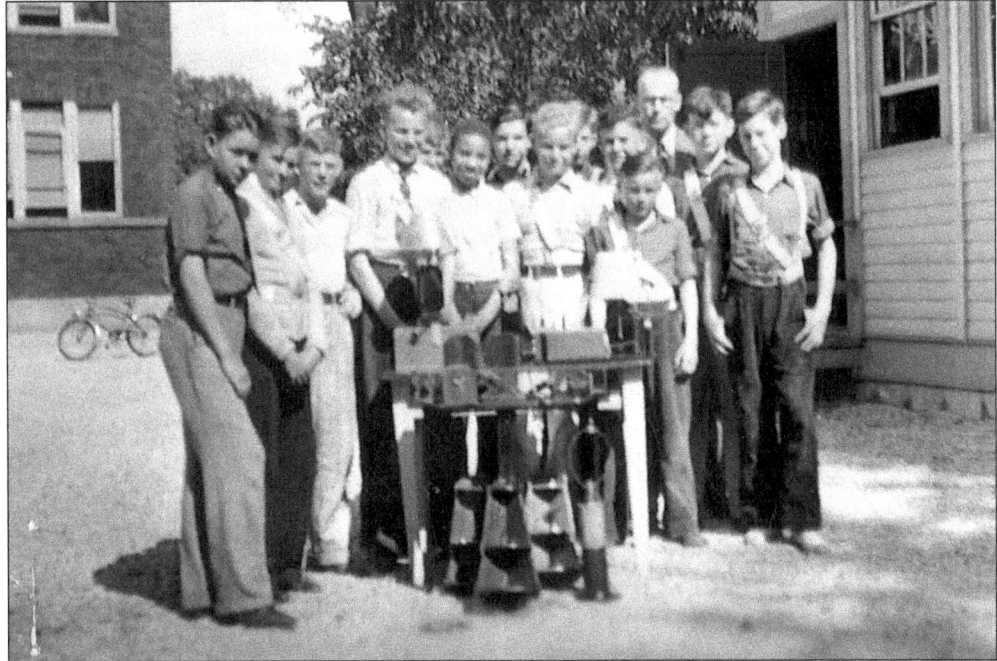

MR. WHITTAKER'S SHOP CLASS AT SCHOOL 85. Mr. Whittaker (standing in the back) and his class show off their creations at school 85 in one of the portable classrooms that was built to accommodate the surplus students. (Courtesy of Bea Cottom.)

OUR LADY OF LOURDES CATHOLIC SCHOOL. From the onset of the establishment of Our Lady of Lourdes Catholic Church in Irvington, education was always a big part of its mission. This photograph shows the parishioners laying the cornerstone for the new school building in 1958. The Amos Butler property was purchased in order to provide additional ground for the school. (Courtesy of Our Lady of Lourdes Catholic Church.)

OUR LADY OF LOURDES SCHOOL DEDICATION. The present school building was dedicated at the beginning of the 1958–1959 school year by pastor Archbishop Paul Schulte. This photograph was taken from the entry hall of the building. (Courtesy of Our Lady of Lourdes Catholic Church.)

MAY CROWNING, 1955. One of the highlights of the Catholic school's year is the May Crowning ceremony where girls dress up in older versions of first communion dresses and veils. This group of girls, probably eighth graders, poses for a photograph along with a statue of the Virgin Mary. According to the notation on the back of the photograph, the boys of Our Lady of Lourdes school did not want to be in the picture. Pictured are Barbara Greener, Patricia Porter, Rita Rhodes, Kathy Mobley, Sandra Heaver, Jan White, Julianna O'Connell, Prudence Rowley, Maureen Burke, Carolyn Koors, Dorothy Schwieters, Marisue Deery, Diana Flanagan, ? Waugh, Sonya Mathson, Alicia Ehrmantrout, Janis Rasche, Phyllis Winkler, Barbara Sanders, Jackie Corey, Mary Jo Gootie, Margie Peague, Pat Walsh, Pat Ley, Kathy Dwyer, Nancy Newman, and Mary Louise Rice. (Courtesy of Our Lady of Lourdes Catholic Church.)

Thomas Carr Howe
High School
Indianapolis Ind.
Thomas Stirling

THOMAS CARR HOWE HIGH SCHOOL, c. 1943. In December 1928, McGuire and Shook Architects was given the authority to begin designing the proposed Irvington High School, but the Depression quickly stalled any talk of a new high school building in the area. The New Deal's Works Progress Administration program provided funding for new schools, so in 1936, the Indianapolis School Board applied for these funds to construct the school; however, it was denied. Indianapolis Public Schools proceeded on its own with local funding, and in 1937, the proposed school was named in honor of Thomas Carr Howe. Ten students registered for the fall semester in 1938, and by September, there were 95 students in the sophomore class and about 350 comprising the freshman class. The illustration at left is by Thomas Stirling. (Above, courtesy of Irvington Historical Society Archives; left, courtesy of Bea Cottom.)

THOMAS CARR HOWE HIGH SCHOOL FACULTY, SEPTEMBER 1938. High school faculty members, from left to right, are (first row) Virginia Childers, Ruby Lou Lillard, Narcie Pollit, Margaret E. Forcht, Mildred Dirks Loew, Janet Keller, Helen B. Allen, Eva F. Abbott, and Mary E. Thumma; (second row) Raphael W. Wolfe, Beldon C. Leonard, Florance C. Guild, Clarence R. Clayton, Charles M. Sharp (principal), George P. Farkas, Helen O'Daniel, Jeff R. Stonex, and E. A. Patterson. (Courtesy of Bea Cottom.)

FRANKLIN COLLEGE PRESS CONVENTION, 1940. Thomas Carr Howe High School students attended a press convention at Franklin College on October 24–26, 1940. Pictured are Roland Crim, Clyde Holder, Miriam Jasper, Ethelda Kieter, Don Clapp, Peg Gordon, Mrs. Griggs, Shirley Courtney, Betty Harvey, Jean Huston, Mary Ellis, Martha Jo Hadley, Mary E. Donnell, Pat Myers, Marilyn Behymer, Kenneth Smith, Virginia Stafford, Betty Stonebraker, Anna Dane Bash, Ann Holloway ?, Melville Weesner, Lois Knapp, and Dot Troutman. (Courtesy of Bea Cottom.)

SENIOR CONSTITUTION COMMITTEE, 1944. From left to right Howard Caldwell Jr., Don Raisco, Joan Bruckman, Florence Guild, Jean Carpenter, Don Auble, and Virginia Reese, members of the Senior Constitution Committee, discuss policies that will help shape their senior year. The committee was one of several student government organizations at the high school. (Courtesy of Bea Cottom.)

CLASS OF 1941'S 25TH ANNIVERSARY. Thomas Carr Howe High School's first graduating class poses for a picture during their 25th anniversary on June 25, 1966. Some of the first students at Howe came from other local high schools, including Tech, Manual, Shortridge, and Washington high schools. This first class had the honor of designing the class ring and deciding whether or not to wear caps and gowns at commencement. (Courtesy of Bea Cottom.)

THE HOWE GOLDEN GIRL, 1963. Being elected the "Howe Golden Girl" or "Brown Boy" for the homecoming court was a great honor. In this photograph, high school principal Thomas Stirling presents varsity cheerleader and senior Diane Elaine Corbin with her circlet and bouquet as the Howe Golden Girl of 1963. At right is Corbin with Brown Boy Nick Von Staden. The dance for the festivities was held in Howe's cafeteria with a bandstand and fountain. The theme of the evening was "autumn haze." Over 500 people attended the semiformal affair. The couple was even featured in the *Indianapolis News*. (Courtesy of Diane Roudebush.)

Howe vs Warren Central

MR. THOMAS STIRLING
PRINCIPAL

LESTER MATHIESON
HEAD COACH

SAMUEL T. KELLEY
ATHLETIC DIRECTOR

HOWE			VISITOR		
NO.	NAME	POS.	NO.	NAME	POS.
37	Mike Albright	E	11	Jon Leavitt*	QB
38	David Marendt	E	12	Jim Beckham	G
39	James Myers	HB	13	Craig Hawks	E
40	Larry Sanborn	G	14	Paul Breuer	G
41	Lonnie Mikolon	HB	15	Don Baker	T
42	Trent Detamore	HB	16	Jonny Cazee	E
43	William Lang	FB	17	Larry Wetherald	QB
44	Stan Bradley	G	18	Rick Guyer	QB
45	Larry Bishop	QB	19	Ronnie Young*	FB
46	Steve Day	E	20	Don Wilson	HB
47	Ray Pier	E	21	Bruce Little*	HB
48	Steve West	HB	22	Chip McClintock	G
49	Ronald Russell	HB	23	Earl Jackson	G
50	Bruce Spear	E	24	Ron Breeden	G
51	Tom Ott	HB	25	John Woodburn	HB
52	Byron Bayne	HB	26	Tom Sponcil*	E
53	Alan Wilkins	G	27	Eddie Clemaer	T
54	Phillip Love	E	28	Tom Fenrimore	G
55	Barry Wenzler	G	29	Bob Sharp	C
56	Brent Anderson	E	30	Bill Burgess	FB
57	Steve West	QB	31	Harry Monroe	FB
58	Steve Gibbs	C	32	Jim Horton	FB
59	George Adams	G	33	Stanley Taylor	HB
60	Richard Ulrey	E	34	Larry Dilk	C
61	John Richardson	C	35	Gunars Janelsins*	G
62	John Fox	HB	36	Steve Stroeh*	T
63	William Greaver	T	37	Janis Janelsins	T
64	Steve Grubbs	G	38	Jack Dyer	T
65	Steve Raasch	T	39	Roger Casey	G
66	James Stewart	FB	40	Steve Fischer	E
67	Richard Schubert	QB	41	Harry Preston	C
68	Kenny Hughes	FB	42	Bob Bechett	T
69	Ronald Bowling	T	43	Bob Baker	T
70	William Evans	T	51	Don Charnetski	FB
71	Robert Adkins	T	55	Dwight Steele	HB
72	Scott Klein	C			

* Returning Lettermen

Principal .... Thomas Stirling
Athletic Dir. . Samuel T. Kelley
Head Coach . Lester Mathieson
Asst. Coach .... Ken Long
Asst. Coach .... Ron Miller
Asst. Coach .... Dave Stewart
Asst. Coach-Harrison Richardson

Principal ... Edward H. Caddy
Athletic Dir. . William E. Glesing
Head Coach .... Dave Shaw
Asst. Coach .... Walt Wintin
Asst. Coach .... Paul Conwell
Asst. Coach ..... Leo Hine

THOMAS CARR HOWE FOOTBALL PROGRAM, 1963. Fans of Thomas Carr Howe High School's football team could not wait to see their team in action under the Friday night lights. This 1963 program is for Howe's game with Warren Central, another east-side high school. The program is peppered with team statistics and announcements by local advertisers who supported Howe throughout its years as Irvington's high school. (Courtesy of Diane Roudebush.)

HOWE HORNETS BASKETBALL TEAM, 1964. The 1964 basketball team included Chuck Mundy, Brent Anderson, Jon Reynolds, Jim Pettee, Ric Burrell, Dick Britton, Craig Carey, Mike Noland, Don Kingery, Bill Cooke, Tom Ott, and coach Jim Stutz. (Courtesy of Diane Roudebush.)

HOWE DRAMA PROGRAM, 1964. The senior class performance of *If a Man Answers* was held on Friday, May 15, 1964, in Thomas Carr Howe High School's auditorium. The auditorium was a recent addition to the building and was a state-of-the-art venue at the time. Howe has opened the doors of the auditorium to other schools and local events that have needed a facility for their own performances, including the neighboring Catholic high school, Scecina Memorial. (Courtesy of Diane Roudebush.)

PREMIERE DRAMA PERFORMANCE

in the New Howe Auditoirum

THE SENIOR CLASS

OF 1964

OF

THOMAS CARR HOWE HIGH SCHOOL

presents

IF A MAN ANSWERS

FRIDAY
MAY 15, 1964

The Senior Class

of

Thomas Carr Howe High School

announces the

Twenty-fourth Annual Commencement Exercises

Wednesday evening, June third

Nineteen hundred and sixty-four

at six-thirty o'clock

Thomas Carr Howe High School Campus

GRADUATION ANNOUNCEMENT, 1964. This is the typical announcement used for a Howe graduation ceremony in the 1960s. On June 3, 1964, the senior class of Thomas Carr Howe High School gathered to celebrate its commencement. The invocation was delivered by Rev. Theodore W. Mikolon, and L. Robert Mottern presented the diplomas to the 368 graduates. The senior prom was held that evening at the Indiana Roof. (Courtesy of Diane Roudebush.)

COMMENCEMENT PROGRAM, 1965. By the mid-1990s, Thomas Carr Howe High School had been on the Indianapolis Public School closure list several times. Although the school escaped being closed in the past, the 1994 winter school board meeting that announced the official closing of Howe was met with sadness by the students and alums in attendance. Seniors vowed to make their last year a year to remember, and many former students came back to see one last basketball game before the doors were closed, presumably forever. The last Thomas Carr Howe High School graduation occurred on June 1, 1995. Five years later, the school was reopened, ushering in a new era for the Irvington high school. Today the building is known as T. C. Howe Academy and accepts students in grades 9 through 12. At the first commencement ceremony after the reopening, members of the school's first graduating class were in attendance. (Courtesy of Diane Roudebush.)

Six

THE PEOPLE

Those who live within the boundaries of Irvington have a name like no other when it comes to describing who they are and where they are from. They are "Irvingtonians," and while the expression hardly dates back to the earliest residents, it is an expression that ties the community of today with the people—famous, infamous, and ordinary—of yesteryear.

Irvington's people are an eclectic group, ranging from scholars and academics to politicians, artists, musicians, builders, spiritual leaders, and a variety of the noteworthy individuals and newsmakers living side by side with doctors, lawyers, homemakers, and teachers. Newsman Howard Caldwell Jr. lived near artist Clifton Wheeler and Dr. John Kingsbury.

Buildings, schools, churches, and stately homes were not enough to keep the community viable, but it was the people who held to the belief that Irvington was a town that offered opportunity to everyone regardless of one's socioeconomic class.

Some names are synonymous with Irvington education, such as Butler, Burgess, Benton, and Howe, while others are remembered for their work with newspapers, like Hilton U. Brown and Kin Hubbard. Some are honored for their creative works, such as William Forsyth and other members of the Irvington Group of artists.

Other names travel in smaller circles, such as Francis "Chief" Belzer, who was known for his work with the Boy Scouts of America, architect Bennajah Weesner, and a few surnames that are spoken with discretion, such as Stephenson, Holmes, and Dillinger.

With forefathers who helped establish Irvington as the jewel of the Indianapolis east side, today's Irvingtonians are no less important than their predecessors, and as the community evolves into the 21st century, new names will emerge to help write the next chapter in Irvington's rich history.

No matter if they were the foundation on which Irvington was built or if they are residents committed to the spirit of Irvington, each one is vital to the past, present, and future of the Irvington community.

FRANK MCKINNEY (KIN) HUBBARD. Kin Hubbard is best known for creating the Hoosier homespun philosopher "Abe Martin" cartoon character, which appeared daily in the *Indianapolis News* and was syndicated in over 300 other newspapers. This photograph shows Hubbard relaxing on the front porch of his home at Emerson Avenue and Pleasant Run Parkway. (Courtesy Indiana Historical Society.)

HILTON U. BROWN AT HOWE GROUND BREAKING, 1937. Thomas Carr Howe High School's first principal, C. M. Sharp, along with Hilton U. Brown and Mrs. Louis Bruck, president of the Irvington Union of Clubs, get ready for the high school ground breaking on May 25, 1937. Brown was known for his work as president of the board of trustees at Butler University as well as for his longtime association with the *Indianapolis News.* (Courtesy of Bea Cottom.)

WILLIAM FORSYTH AND FRIENDS. The date of this photograph is unknown, but pictured second from right is William Forsyth, a prominent Irvington artist showing his musical talents in a costumed skit. He was born in California, Ohio, in 1854 but moved to Indianapolis with his family in 1860. He attended the Indiana School of Art and studied overseas for a bit. After returning to Indiana, Forsyth became prominent as one of the "Hoosier Group" of impressionist painters. (Courtesy of Irvington Historical Society Archives.)

FRANCIS "CHIEF" BELZER. Francis "Chief" Belzer (center, kneeling on the ground) plants a walnut tree, a gift of the Mount Vernon Daughters of the American Revolution commemorating the George Washington bicentennial celebration on May 15, 1932. Belzer's name is synonymous with Scouting. He organized Troop 9 at the Irvington United Methodist Church. (Courtesy of Irvington Presbyterian Church.)

DAVID CURTIS (D. C.) STEPHENSON, 1935. Born in Houston, Texas, on August 21, 1891, D. C. Stephenson was the grand dragon of the Ku Klux Klan in Indiana and king kleagle of seven other states. As one of the more successful leaders of the movement, he acquired wealth and power in the political realm and had his personal friends elected to some of the highest offices in the state. He was responsible for the abduction and rape of Madge Oberholtzer, which led to her death on April 14, 1925. He was convicted and sentenced to life in prison, though he was paroled twice. He left prison for the final time on December 22, 1956, and moved to Johnson City, Tennessee, where he died on June 28, 1966. (Left, courtesy of Robert Van Buskirk; below, courtesy of Tiffany Photography Studio, Gary Yohler and Bob Raleigh.)

INDIANA HOTEL REGISTRY, MARCH 16, 1925. Stephenson registered himself and Oberholtzer under the names "Mr. and Mrs. W. B. Morgan" of Franklin when he abducted the statehouse worker and went to Hammond, Indiana. The couple stayed in room 416 with Stephenson's bodyguard, Earl Gentry, in the next room. The following day, Oberholtzer poisoned herself in hopes that Stephenson would return her to her family in Indianapolis. (Courtesy of Robert Van Buskirk.)

OBERHOLTZER FUNERAL PROCESSION, APRIL 1925. After Oberholtzer poisoned herself, Stephenson returned her to Indianapolis but kept her hidden in a room above his carriage house in Irvington. She was eventually returned to her family, but by that time, her health had deteriorated. Before dying a month after the ordeal, Oberholtzer gave a deathbed statement that led to Stephenson's conviction. Oberholtzer died on April 14, 1925. (Courtesy of Robert Van Buskirk.)

THE ROBERTSON FAMILY, C. 1911. Rev. David A. Robertson (in hat) gazes upon his grandson Frank Robertson sitting on Roberta Robinson's lap outside his home at 65 North Ritter Avenue. Frank was a doctor who practiced medicine in the attic of the home. The family was also elder members of the Irvington United Methodist Church. (Courtesy of Mark and Cathy Kippert.)

BENNAJAH WEESNER. Bennajah Weesner was the architect of the original Irvington Presbyterian Church building. He also designed a number of other churches throughout Indiana. According to church records, he refused all payment for his work on the redbrick church and when the trustees insisted, he donated his income to the building fund for the church. (Courtesy of Irvington Presbyterian Church.)

WILLIAM THOMAS MCVEY, C. 1915.
William Thomas McVey was known as a
builder of many Irvington homes along
Downey Avenue, but he also played a tuba in
the Irvington band, which often performed
on Irving Circle. He was a charter member
of the Irvington Odd Fellows, being initiated
in 1909. McVey died on April 13, 1922,
and is buried at Memorial Park Cemetery
on East Washington Street. (Courtesy of
Lori Malander.)

THE CALDWELL FAMILY, 1948. Elsie (Felt) Caldwell, Howard C. Caldwell Sr., and Virginia
Caldwell were the immediate family members of newsman Howard Caldwell Jr. and longtime
Irvington residents. Howard Sr. and Virginia met while attending Butler College in Irvington,
and she also became a Butler student on the Fairview campus. The family lived at 81 North
Hawthorne Lane. (Courtesy of Howard Caldwell Jr.)

IRVINGTON PAGEANT IN ELLENBERGER PARK, C. 1915. Marjorie Hall and Dora Bosart dress up as Native Americans for an episode in the Irvington pageant that was held in Ellenberger Park to celebrate Indiana's settlement. The park provided a wealth of social opportunities for the Irvington community and had a natural amphitheater to accommodate many people. (Courtesy of Marge Conly.)

GEORGE RUSSELL AND FAMILY, C. 1905. George Russell ran the Irvington train depot and also served as a telegraph officer and a postmaster. He eventually became involved in real estate and had an office above the Irvington Bank building at Ritter Avenue and Washington Street. This photograph was taken in the backyard of 60 North Ritter Avenue. (Courtesy of Larry Muncie.)

IRVINGTON DRAMATIC CLUB, 1926. Bernice and Elbert Glass dressed up as George and Martha Washington for a dramatic club "Colonial evening." The Irvington Dramatic Club was a successor to the Sheridan Dramatic Club and was organized in 1914. Throughout the Irvington community, there were many clubs and organizations, including the Irvington Women's Club, established in 1892; the Tuesday Club; and the Fortnightly Club. (Courtesy of Marge Conly.)

IRVINGTON DRAMATIC CLUB PROGRAM. On February 15, 1969, the Irvington Dramatic Club presented Neil Simon's *Come Blow Your Horn* in school 77's auditorium. The club continued until 1976 and included members such as Jean Melvin, Bill Woods, Hariette Baker, and Erle A. Kightlinger. (Courtesy of Howard Caldwell Jr.)

GUEST MEETING

The Irvington Dramatic Club

presents

COME BLOW YOUR HORN

A Comedy in Three Acts
by Neil Simon

Director - Jo Money

School 77 Auditorium
February 15, 1969 - 8:30 P.M.

Hosts: Officers of the Club

THE HALL GIRLS. Bernice Hall (Glass) and Marjorie Hall (Montgomery) sit with their dog at their home on Downey Avenue. At 14 months apart in age, many people thought the girls were twins. They were in the same grade at school due to Bernice having had a case of typhoid fever in early childhood. The girls had many family connections in Irvington, including William Forsyth and the Layman family. They were members of the Daughters of the American Revolution through one of their Hume family relations, who was Gen. George Washington's surveyor. The Hall girls attended Butler College, each graduating in 1915 with a degree in home economics. They pledged Kappa Alpha Theta and were also charter members of the Irvington Dramatic Club. The girls were always encouraged to be well educated. Their grandmother moved to Irvington from the family farm in Trafalgar with her four children so they could be educated beyond the sixth grade. They all became graduates of Butler, and the tradition of higher education was passed on. (Courtesy of Marge Conly.)

HOWARD CALDWELL JR. Known throughout Indianapolis for his 40 years in broadcast journalism, Howard Caldwell Jr. spent his early years living at the Audubon Court Apartments on the corner of Washington Street and Audubon Road next door to the Layman house. When the Depression hit, his family moved into his grandfather Caldwell's home on Bosart Avenue, but eventually his parents bought a home on Hawthorne Lane where he lived until he joined the navy in 1944. He attended elementary school at school 57 and served as a paper carrier for the *Indianapolis News*. He is a Thomas Carr Howe High School and Butler University graduate. Although his days of living in Irvington were over after high school, he consistently found himself drawn back to the community not only in productions of the Irvington Dramatic Club but also as a member of the Irvington Historical Society. He recalled his Irvington memories as part of his broadcast stories. (Courtesy of Howard Caldwell Jr.)

HANGING OUT ON HAWTHORNE LANE, 1917. Taken from the porch of 29 North Hawthorne Lane, John Dobyns and Howard Campbell, both students at school 57, pose for a photograph on a summer's day. Note the undeveloped land in the background. According to the notation, the field usually held cows, but one day the cows ended up on the front lawn of Our Lady of Lourdes Catholic Church. (Courtesy of Larry Muncie.)

THE UNSAFETY COACH LINE. Out to capitalize on public transportation and make some money with 1¢ fares, Bernard Korbly Jr. (left), John Korbly (both sitting at the top) Victor Jose (behind the wheel) and Bob Glass (pushing) developed the Union Attraction Company to serve the transportation needs of Irvington youth in the 1920s. (Courtesy of Marge Conly.)

MARGE GLASS. Girl Scouting was very popular in Irvington with the Irvington Presbyterian Church serving as home to the first Girl Scout troop in Indianapolis. Marge Glass was the daughter of Bernice and Elbert Glass and the sister of Bob Glass. A graduate of Shortridge High School, she was very active in Girl Scout Troop 57, where her mother served as a leader. (Courtesy of Marge Conly.)

THE IRVINGTON NEEDLE CLUB, JUNE 1942. The Irvington Needle Club was a local hobby club. Once a month women of the community met at a member's home to crochet, knit, quilt, and darn. Pictured from left to right are Nancy Carr, Nellie Martin, Anna Cronin, Pearl Krause, Bessie Richmond, Mary Kaltwasser, Thelma Whatts, Minnie Mountjoy, Elizabeth Gadberry, and Christie Holland. (Courtesy of Bob Montgomery.)

IRVINGTON IN WORLD WAR I. Irvington was active on both the home front and the battlefield during World War I and World War II. Pictured are Ralph (left) and Arthur Harder with their mother on the lawn of her Emerson Avenue home. Arthur served as a captain in the American Expeditionary Force in France, and while his brother Ralph was too young to join the military during the war, he ultimately joined the navy when the war ended. (Courtesy of Irvington Historical Society Archives.)

WORLD WAR II. Our Lady of Lourdes Catholic Church parishioner Harry F. Dalton attended the 9th Service Command School at Camp Adair, Oregon, having joined the army in 1943. He was discharged on February 17, 1946, after serving overseas in the European Theater. (Courtesy of Harry Dalton family.)

Seven

THE LANDMARKS

From its early days in the late 19th century to the beginning of the new millennium, Irvington has been supported by the residents and businesses that call Irvington home. Although the names and faces have changed over the years, and growth on the east side once inhibited the neighborhood, Irvington constantly evolves to meet any challenge with a community spirit that is second to none.

From public buildings to a thriving medical center, green space, and numerous commercial establishments often owned by proprietors who grew up in Irvington, the town still remains committed to the autonomous identity first conceived by Jacob Julian and Sylvester Johnson in 1870. As a nationally recognized and locally protected historic district, Irvington takes pains to ensure that home renovation is consistent with the historic nature of the area, new buildings maintain the look of the established storefronts, and the special history of this neighborhood is preserved for all to enjoy.

While some of the original buildings are lost to time and others are a mere ghost of what they used to be, many remain along with new landmarks that have been built and will stay firmly etched in the minds of generations for years to come. With the churches, homes, and schools leading the way, the local businesses also have a high standard to maintain as part of the landscape that is Irvington.

Although Washington Street was not originally considered to be the commercial hub of Irvington, over time, it became the main drag of the community and, as railroad traffic became less significant, the original commercial structures around the site of the old depot suffered. The more time goes by, the older buildings take on various incarnations never considered by the original architects.

In the great spirit of other Indianapolis neighborhoods known for their retro style such as Broad Ripple, Lockerbie Square, and Woodruff Place, Irvington does not sacrifice the past in order to stay in the present. Rather, Irvington stays true to itself by using its history to move forward.

IRVINGTON HISTORIC DISTRICT MAP. This map shows the boundary of the Irvington Historic District. Portions of Emerson Avenue, Pleasant Run Parkway, Arlington Avenue, and the original Irvington plat are all encompassed in this map that was illustrated in the Indiana Historic Sites and Structures Inventory. (Courtesy of Irvington Historical Society Archives.)

AERIAL VIEW OF IRVINGTON, 1925. Taken by Dr. John Kingsbury from an airplane, this aerial view of Irvington looks east on Michigan Street. Unlike the original overview of Irvington in 1881, there are many more structures dotting the landscape, although there is still plenty of open space. (Courtesy of Larry Muncie.)

MARION COUNTY CHILDREN'S GUARDIANS HOME. Relocated to University Avenue in 1898, the Marion County Children's Guardians Home made Irvington its permanent site after moving from South State Street. While the neighborhood could not have been more perfect for the home, the initial structure almost immediately proved to be too small. By 1915, there were safety issues as well. Later that year, the building was destroyed by fire, and the 55 children living there were placed in local homes until the new building, shown below, was completed in 1916. (Courtesy of Indiana Historical Society Bass Collection.)

THE IRVINGTON FIRE DEPARTMENT. Station No. 25 was established in 1903, but the building designed to protect the neighborhood from disaster caught fire not long after it was built. The firemen extinguished the fire, and the building was repaired and served the Irvington area for many years. (Courtesy of Indiana Historical Society Bass Collection.)

THE IRVINGTON PRINT SHOP, C. 1900. Operated by Edward Hecker (left), an established writer and printer, this print shop was located at 5215 East Washington Street. Hecker spent a number of years teaching deaf children and was also instrumental in the establishment of Warren Central High School. (Courtesy of Larry Muncie.)

THE IRVING THEATER. Built in 1913, the Irving Theater has seen many incarnations over the years. A second story was added to the building in the 1920s, and as multiplex theaters became all the rage and neighborhood matinees seemed old fashioned, owners divided the theater in half in order to create two screens. Residents during the 1940s remember when a war tax increased the price of a movie by 1¢, which meant that many children had to do extra chores to earn their movie money. Today the Irving is a live-performance venue featuring many local and regional acts. (Courtesy of Larry Muncie.)

THE KILE OAK. An unusual landmark in Irvington is the Kile oak, a large bur oak tree estimated by foresters to be about 400 years old. The tree sits at 5939 Beechwood Avenue and has been preserved in a natural setting since 1973. The tree is named for Rev. Oliver Kile, who was the first person to build a home on the lot. His funeral was held under the tree in 1924. (Courtesy of Irvington Historical Society Archives.)

THE IRVINGTON MASONIC LODGE NO. 666. The cornerstone for this unique building was laid on December 10, 1921. Construction was not completed until the following year. This photograph shows the building before the front entrance was completed. (Courtesy of Larry Muncie.)

INTERIOR OF IRVINGTON MASONIC LODGE. Before the lodge building was completed, the Masons met in many other locations around the community. Lodge buildings of the era commonly had commercial space on the first floor in order to provide support for the lodge, which met on the second floor. For example, the Irvington Post Office was located within the lodge building until 1950. (Courtesy of Irvington Historical Society Archives.)

EASTERN STAR OFFICERS, 1939. The Irvington Masonic Lodge was also home to a chapter of the Eastern Star. From left to right, the officers for 1939 included (first row) Nancy Carr, Myrtle Flynn, Dorothy Montgomery, Ruby Downard, Florence Mountjoy, and Elsie Stone; (second row) Christie Holland, Mary Kaltwasser, Elmer Mullin, Omel Curry, Elena Riffle, Ann Burns, Ida Snedaker, Nellie Mullin, Frank Mountjoy, Estella Foley, and Venera Smith. (Courtesy of Bob Mongomery.)

WHITTIER PHARMACY. Among the many shops along Washington Street, Irvington had its fair share of drugstores and pharmacies throughout the years. This emporium, the Whittier Place Pharmacy, was located west of the Irvington Fire Station at a time when the National Road still sported trolley car tracks. (Courtesy of Irvington Historical Society Archives.)

PUBLIC TRANSPORTATION IN IRVINGTON. Electric trolleys such as the one pictured here, marked "East Washington-Sheridan," transported people from throughout the Irvington community to downtown Indianapolis. Later there was a turnaround for buses at Emerson Avenue and Washington Street. Children playing on Brown's Hill were admonished to watch for traffic as their snow sleds sometimes landed on the National Road. (Courtesy of Indiana Historical Society.)

Brown Branch Library. When the Bona Thompson Memorial Library opened its doors, it not only served Butler University but it also served the community as a public lending library until World War I. A home adjacent to school 57 became the temporary library until a new branch was built 30 years later. It was named for Hilton U. Brown. Today the building is an early childhood center. (Courtesy Irvington Historical Society Archives.)

Irving Circle Park Fountain Rebuilding, 1970s. When the time came to rebuild the fountain in Irving Circle Park, the community pitched in to create a structure worthy of its predecessors. This photograph shows the neighborhood gathered together as the foundation for the new fountain is constructed. (Courtesy of Larry Muncie.)

IRVINGTON ICE AND COAL COMPANY. Completed in 1915, the location near the Baltimore and Ohio Railroad at 400 South Ritter Avenue proved advantageous for receiving ice and coal deliveries. Until the days when everyone benefited from electric refrigeration, ice and coal companies such as this one were essential businesses for any community. Thomas Carr Howe was the first president of the firm. (Courtesy of Robert Van Buskirk.)

THE JIFFY COMPANY, C. 1965. Jeff Johnson stands outside the Jiffy Building west of Our Lady of Lourdes Catholic Church on East Washington Street. The primary product was Jiffy, a chemical drain cleaner that was eventually renamed Lik-Wid Plumr. In the late 1960s, Clorox purchased the rights to the cleaner for approximately $18.2 million. (Author's collection.)

ELMER R. MULLIN TIN SHOP, 1939. Elmer R. Mullin was the area tinsmith, roofer, and furnace man. Located at 5517 Bonna Avenue, the tin shop was the site for the fabrication of furnace pipes, heat boxes, gutters, and other tin metal forms. The shop was established in 1924 and remained in business until Mullin's death in 1943. (Courtesy of Bob Montgomery.)

COMMUNITY HOSPITAL BUS FUND-RAISER, C. 1951. In a grassroots effort to raise money for a hospital on the east side, the members of the Community Hospital board solicited businesses and private citizens to help build the new hospital. The effort was considered to be one of the most effective and swiftest campaigns of the day. (Courtesy of Community Health Network.)

VICE PRESIDENT NIXON AT COMMUNITY HOSPITAL. In 1954, the groundbreaking ceremony for Community Hospital was attended by Vice Pres. Richard M. Nixon. Through community efforts alone, many of which came from Irvington residents, the hospital acquired the first $9 million toward the hospital building at Sixteenth Street and Ritter Avenue. (Courtesy of Community Health Network.)

COMMUNITY HOSPITAL AUXILIARY. The auxiliary was started by a guild of 150 women organized by the president of the Irvington Woman's Club. The ladies not only solicited funds for the hospital, as shown here, but they also sewed draperies for patient rooms. (Courtesy of Community Health Network.)

IRVINGTON AT HALLOWEEN. Halloween has always been a special time in Irvington, even before the first Halloween festival in 1946. Pictured above, Billy Butler, Bobby Montgomery, Phyllis ?, Charles Davis, Jimmy Davis, and Alvira Whitter pose for a photograph in their Halloween costumes outside of 203 South Ritter Avenue in 1941. During the last weekend before Halloween, Washington Street shuts down for the Halloween festival (below), during which business owners allow children to paint on store windows, and a costumed parade is held with local children showing off their Halloween creations. The event is attended by between 5,000 and 10,000 people each year not only from Irvington but also from surrounding communities. Coupled with the Haunted Irvington Tour, the town knows how to make the most of the fall season. (Above, courtesy of Bob Montgomery; below, courtesy of Judy Kosegi.)

ELLENBERGER PARK POOL SWIM TEAM. Ellenberger Park has been a local hangout for youths in the Irvington area since its inception thanks to the aquatics center and neighborhood ice rink. In this photograph (from left to right) assistant swim coach Ann Boren, Bill St. John, Jim Surface, and assistant coach Dan Dunbar practice for a local meet. (Courtesy of Tiffany Photography Studio, Gary Yohler and Bob Raleigh.)

MEMORIAL DAY COOKOUT, MAY 29, 1978. Pictured from left to right are author Julie (Johnson) Young, 5, standing with her brother Bruce Johnson, 10, and cousin Tracy (Denton) Silvers, 7, in the backyard of 5829 Oak Avenue in Irvington. Irvington families often gather for private celebrations. (Author's collection.)

BIBLIOGRAPHY

Diebold, Paul. *Greater Irvington: Architecture, People and Places on the Indianapolis East Side.* Indianapolis: Irvington Historical Society, 1997.

Diebold, Paul, Julia Fangmeier, and Ian McCrae. *Mission Accomplished.* Indianapolis: Irvington Historical Society, 1995.

Hunter, Alan E., and Russ Simnick. *Irvington Haunts.* Westfield, IN: Haunted Publishing, 2004.

Muncie, Larry. *Irvington Stories.* Indianapolis: Irvington Historical Society, 1992.

———. *Irvington Album: A Collection of Historic Photographs of the Irvington Community.* Indianapolis: Irvington Historical Society, 1994.

Waller, George MacGregor. *Butler University: A Sesquicentennial Celebration.* Bloomington , IN: Indiana University Press, 2006.

Winders, Gertrude Hecker. *A Glimpse of Irvington Then and Now 1870–1970.* Indianapolis: Irvington Historical Society, 1970.

www.420.ips.k12.in.us/Howe+History/default.aspx

www.butler.edu

Visit us at
arcadiapublishing.com

www.ingramcontent.com/pod-product-compliance
Lightning Source LLC
Chambersburg PA
CBHW050633110426
42813CB00007B/1797